Crete 1941

Germany's lightning airborne assault

Campaign • 147

Crete 1941

Germany's lightning airborne assault

Peter D Antill • Illustrated by Howard Gerrard

Series editor Lee Johnson • *Consultant editor* David G Chandler

First published in Great Britain in 2005 by Osprey Publishing,
Midland House, West Way, Botley, Oxford OX2 0PH, UK
44-02 23rd St, Suite 219, Long Island City, NY 11101, USA
Email: info@ospreypublishing.com

Transferred to digital print on demand 2011

First published 2005
6th impression 2010

Printed and bound by PrintOnDemand-Worldwide.com Peterborough, UK

A CIP catalogue record for this book is available from the British Library

ISBN: 978 1 84176 844 1

Editorial by Lee Johnson
Design by The Black Spot
Index by Bob Munro
Maps by The Map Studio
3D bird's-eye views by The Black Spot
Battlescene artwork by Howard Gerrard
Originated by PPS Grasmere Ltd., Leeds, UK
Typeset in Helvetica Neue and ITC New Baskerville

Author's acknowledgements

I would like to thank Heather Mathie, Anna Taiki and the staff of the Alexander Turnbull Library in Wellington, New Zealand,
as well as Yvonne Oliver and the staff of the photographic department of the Imperial War Museum, for allowing me to use the
photographs reproduced in this publication. In a similar vein, I would like to thank John Dillon and Brian L. Davis for their efforts
in sending me a number of photographs from their own personal collections that helped immensely in the production of this book.
  A big thank you goes to Ken Ford, Steven Zaloga, Bruce Quarrie and Gordon Williamson for their helpful comments and
encouragement, as well as to the series editor Lee Johnson, for his patience and encouragement during this, my first book for
Osprey. A final thank you goes to my wife Michelle, my parents David and Carole, and my parents-in-law, Sally and Alan for
their patience and encouragement during my own 'Battle for Crete' – the writing of this book!

Author's note

Both historical and modern texts include numerous English language variations of the names of many of the towns and villages
on Crete. In the interests of clarity I have tried to adopt the most commonly used modern version throughout the book.
  Many of the numerous published books, articles, manuscripts and online sources disagree about the timing of certain events
or the identities and locations of particular units. I have tried as far as possible to reconcile the different accounts but apologise
in advance for any errors that have survived.

Artist's note

Readers may care to note that the original paintings from which the colour plates in this book were prepared are available for
private sale. All reproduction copyright whatsoever is retained by the Publisher. Enquiries should be addressed to:

Howard Gerrard, 11 Oaks Road, Tenterden, Kent, TN30 6RD, UK

The Publishers regret that they can enter into no correspondence upon this matter.

The Woodland Trust

Osprey Publishing is supporting the Woodland Trust, the UK's leading woodland conservation charity, by funding the
dedication of trees.

www.ospreypublishing.com

Key to military series symbols

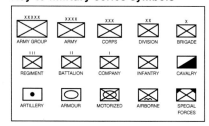

CONTENTS

INTRODUCTION

The German invasion of Crete in May 1941 stands as a landmark in the history of airborne warfare. Until that point, airborne operations had been used mainly in a tactical and operational context to seize key objectives in advance of the ground forces, such as the seizure on 26 April 1941 during the Balkan campaign of the bridge over the Corinth Canal, and the seizure of the Belgium fortress of Eban Emael on the 11 May 1940. The German invasion of Crete, codenamed Operation *Merkur*, or *Mercury*, after the Roman god of communication, travel and theft – the counterpart of Hermes, the messenger of the gods in Greek mythology – remains the only operation in history in which a major strategic objective was assaulted and secured exclusively by airborne troops. The operation was the brainchild of Generalmajor Kurt Student, the commander and dedicated champion of the airborne forces (the Fallschirmjäger), who firmly believed that the paratroopers were capable of operating in their own right and not merely as a tool to support the Wehrmacht.

The immediate background to Operation *Mercury* lies in the events in Europe, and particularly the Balkans, during 1940 and 1941. With the postponement of Operation *Seelöwe* (*Sealion*), the planned invasion of Britain, Hitler decided to opt for a peripheral strategy as recommended by others in the Nazi hierarchy such as Reichsmarschall Hermann Göring and Grossadmiral Erich Raeder. The aim was to bring Britain to the negotiating table before American assistance could prove effective, or the Soviet Union decided to enter the war on the Allied side. Even the army considered a Mediterranean strategy with the Chief of Staff, General Franz Halder discussing options with General Walter von Brauchitsch, in case *Seelöwe* proved impossible. In October 1940, Hitler attempted to cement a Mediterranean coalition by travelling on his personal train to visit General Franco, Spain's Nationalist dictator, at Hendaye and Marshal Pétain, President of Vichy France – the only time Hitler left his headquarters for anybody other than Il Duce, a sign that he attached a great deal of importance to the plan. Neither meeting was entirely successful – Hitler's meeting with Franco drawing a comment from Hitler that he would rather have several teeth removed – as both leaders were wary of losing colonial territory in order to persuade the other to join the Axis cause. These diplomatic efforts were designed to allow the Wehrmacht to conduct an assault on Gibraltar (Operation *Felix*), then deploy reinforcements to aid the Italian forces in Libya (an offer made personally to Mussolini) enabling Axis forces to drive for the Suez Canal.

Hitler had in fact vetoed earlier Italian designs on Yugoslavia as it was tied economically to the Reich, and he wanted to keep the Balkans relatively stable. He had intervened in a dispute between Hungary and Romania over the region of Transylvania, as Germany depended upon

OPPOSITE, TOP **Queuing for food (as evidenced by the mess tins held by the soldier in the foreground) at a mess arranged for the Signals Section of the New Zealand Divisional Headquarters, located somewhere near Hania, soon after their arrival on Crete in May 1941. (Alexander Turnbull Library, DA-13085)**

OPPOSITE, BOTTOM **Corporal Cook (who has the pipe) along with other members of New Zealand 1st Machine Gun Company soon after their arrival on the island in early May 1941 – photographed by H.R. Hall. (Alexander Turnbull Library, DA-14274)**

Romanian oil exports, and while he had allowed the transfer of some territory to Hungary (Hitler also settled the Bulgarian claim for Southern Dobrudja), he had guaranteed the remainder of Romania and sent a large military 'training mission' to the country. This upset the Soviets who had seen that part of the Balkans as traditionally in their sphere of influence, indeed they had annexed part of Romania – Bessarabia and Bukovina – during the Battle for France. Despite German diplomatic assurances, the Soviets accused them of breaching Article III of the Non-Aggression Pact that called for joint consultation.

Having established some form of stability in the Balkans, the Führer strongly recommended to the Italians that the status quo be maintained for the time being. Hitler was anxious that war with the Soviet Union be initiated under circumstances of his own choosing, not as a result of some crisis in the Balkans. This immensely annoyed Mussolini who was afraid that the war might end before the Italian Armed Forces could demonstrate their military prowess to the world. Greece seemed to be the exception to the Balkan rule, as it was technically part of the Mediterranean theatre and could serve as a strategic outpost to support the Italian drive against Egypt and the Suez Canal. Indeed, Hitler had tried to interest Mussolini in both Greece and Crete as early as July 1940. Both OKH (the Army High Command) and OKW (the High Command of the Armed Forces) had considered plans for a joint Italian–German offensive in the Mediterranean and concluded that an attack on Greece would be an essential part of any campaign. Such an attack would take place after the Italian capture of Mersa Matruh, giving the Axis airfields in North Africa from which to provide air support for a drive on Suez and an airborne invasion of Crete. Although the Greek leader, General Metaxas, maintained a neutral position, Greece was bound strategically and economically to Britain, and the Greek royal family had strong British connections. Occupying mainland Greece and Crete would pre-empt a British move into Greece that would directly threaten Italy, provide an additional base for operations against the Italian advance in North Africa and threaten the Romanian oil fields. Therefore an Italian attack on Greece suited Hitler's overall plans, and he may have even given Mussolini a green light when the two met at the Brenner Pass on 4 October.

The Italian intelligence assessment of the Greek Armed Forces was unflattering at best, and therefore an easy victory was confidently predicted. British intervention would be forestalled by Marshal Graziani simultaneously launching the second stage of his North African offensive against Mersa Matruh. Mussolini launched his attack on 28 October after issuing an ultimatum to the Greeks. Unfortunately he had ignored warnings that the Italian forces in Albania were completely unprepared to conduct an autumn campaign and had not even been assigned engineers. The lack of a clear and sensible strategy – such as driving directly on the vital port of Salonika instead of pushing across the mountain range of the Epirus – exasperated Hitler almost as much as the campaign's utterly inefficient and uncoordinated execution. He later stated that he had counselled against undertaking the expedition at that point. The Italian campaign in Greece quickly ground to a complete halt and the Greeks then launched a counter-offensive that drove the Italians out of their country and threatened Albania itself. The Italian position in the eastern

RIGHT **Soldiers from the 2nd New Zealand Expeditionary Force, resting in a village street on Crete. (Alexander Turnbull Library, DA-01157)**

BELOW, RIGHT **British, Australian and New Zealand troops from a variety of units disembark at Souda Bay after their evacuation from Greece after the Balkan campaign in late April 1941. (Alexander Turnbull Library, DA-01611)**

Mediterranean then started to completely unravel. First the British damaged half of the Italian battle fleet in a daring raid on the port of Taranto on 11 November, then they intervened in Greece by sending RAF squadrons there and a battalion of infantry to Crete to secure Souda Bay. The latter move allowed the Greeks to transfer the Cretan V Division to the mainland. In a final blow the British took the initiative in the desert war after Marshal Graziani had stopped at Sidi Barrani to reorganise his supply lines. The British attack completely defeated the Italian force of ten divisions in Libya and threatened the entire Italian position in North Africa.

Troops from the 28th (Maori) Battalion, part of the 2nd NZEF at a transit camp in Egypt on the morning after their evacuation from Crete. (Alexander Turnbull Library, DA-06839)

At the same time as the Italians were facing crisis in the eastern Mediterranean, events elsewhere were to change the context of the situation entirely. The Germans faced continued Soviet intransigence and suspicions over their plans for Europe. Since late July 1940, Hitler had been toying with the idea of exactly when to attack the Soviet Union but had decided to defer the decision to try and secure the Balkan and Mediterranean theatres and, in the process, weaken the UK's position, potentially forcing her to the negotiating table. Hitler therefore considered delaying the attack on the Soviet Union until 1942. Events towards the end of 1940 were to cause an irrevocable eastward shift of the emphasis in the German war effort and bring forward the timetable for the attack on the Soviet Union by a year. In November, the Soviet Foreign Minister, Molotov, visited Berlin for negotiations with Hitler and Von Ribbentrop to pave the way for Soviet membership of the Axis. Despite the Germans dangling the tempting carrot of a share in the British Empire, Molotov would not be deflected from Soviet demands to control Finland and Bulgaria, as well as the exits from the Baltic Sea. Hitler was staggered by the scale of Stalin's demands and decided that the issue of when to attack the Soviet Union had been settled. The Soviet Union had to be destroyed in 1941 before the United States could enter the war decisively. With this decision, the nature of the peripheral strategy changed fundamentally. No longer was it part of the war against Britain, but rather part of the preparations for war against the Soviet Union. The southern flank had to be secured so that the British could not intervene effectively and threaten the Axis position in the Balkans.

In light of these events, and as a result of the new emphasis on an attack on the Soviet Union, the original staff plans for the Mediterranean were revised. Operation *Felix* was put on hold, possibly until late 1942, due to Franco's bland lack of commitment to the Axis cause. However, the invasion of Greece had become more important than ever because of the need to secure the right flank of the advance into the Soviet Union. It would also act as a cover for the deployment of

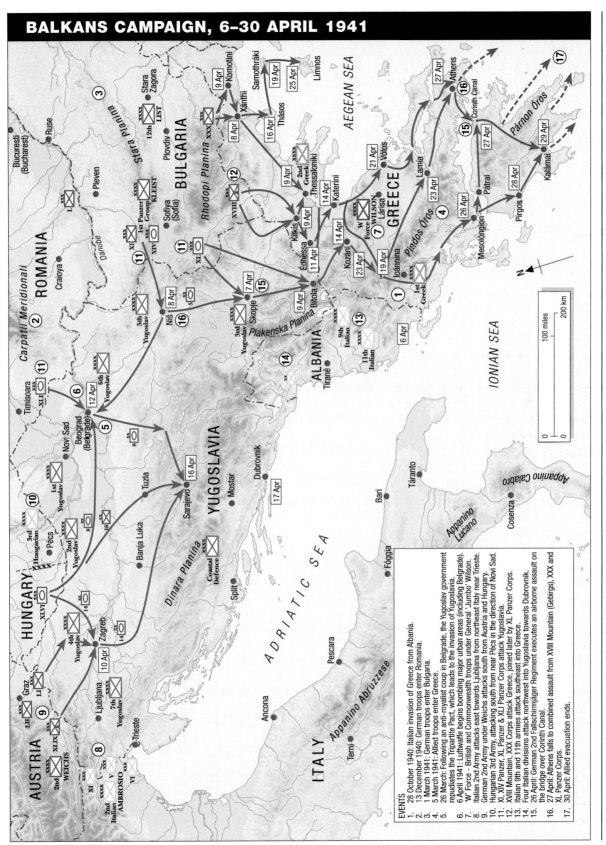

BALKANS CAMPAIGN, 6–30 APRIL 1941

EVENTS

1. 28 October 1940: Italian invasion of Greece from Albania.
2. 13 December 1940: German troops enter Romania.
3. 1 March 1941: German troops enter Bulgaria.
4. 5 March 1941: Allied troops enter Greece.
5. 26 March: Following an anti-royalist coup in Belgrade, the Yugoslav government repudiates the Tripartite Pact, which leads to the invasion of Yugoslavia.
6. 6 April 1941: Luftwaffe begins bombing major urban areas (including Belgrade).
7. 'W' Force – British and Commonwealth troops under General 'Jumbo' Wilson.
8. Italian 2nd Army attacks east towards Ljubljana from northeast Italy near Trieste.
9. German 2nd Army under Weichs attacks south from Austria and Hungary.
10. Hungarian 3rd Army, attacking south from near Pécs in the direction of Novi Sad.
11. XI, XIV Panzer, XL Panzer & XLI Panzer Corps attack Yugoslavia.
12. XVIII Mountain, XXX Corps attack Greece, joined later by XL Panzer Corps.
13. Italian 9th and 11th armies attack southeast into Greece.
14. Four Italian divisions attack northwest into Yugoslavia towards Dubrovnik.
15. 26 April: German 2nd Fallschirmjäger Regiment executes an airborne assault on the bridge over Corinth Canal.
16. 27 April: Athens falls to combined assault from XVIII Mountain (Gebirgs), XXX and XL Panzer Corps.
17. 30 April: Allied evacuation ends.

11

troops eastwards in preparation for Operation *Barbarossa*. In this light, the invasion of Greece can be seen as a limited operation, as was the sending of an expeditionary force, the Afrika Korps under Generalleutnant Erwin Rommel, to North Africa to bolster the Italian defence and contain the British advance. No-one, least of all Hitler, anticipated that Rommel would develop much more ambitious ideas.

Göring and Raeder were both unhappy at the new emphasis on a move eastwards. Both men had wanted to see Britain knocked out of the war before Germany turned its attention east, in order to prevent the dreaded two-front war. Also, in Göring's eyes, the Luftwaffe would probably play a subservient role to the army in *Barbarossa*, but in the Mediterranean, the Luftwaffe would still have freedom of action, and so planning continued for operations against Gibraltar, Malta and Crete – all potential targets of the airborne forces. Fliegerkorps X was transferred from Norway as they specialised in anti-shipping operations and scored their first success by crippling the aircraft carrier HMS *Illustrious* on 10 January.

On 6 April 1941, while preparations were still underway for Operation *Barbarossa*, the Germans invaded both Greece (Operation *Marita*) and Yugoslavia (Operation *Strafe*), where a coup by a group of military officers had toppled the regime that had acceded to German demands and joined the Tripartite Pact. General Archibald Wavell had already despatched an expeditionary force, called 'W' Force after its commander Lieutenant General Henry 'Jumbo' Wilson. It consisted of the British 1st Armoured Brigade (Brigadier Harold Charrington) and the I Anzac Corps (Lieutenant General Sir Thomas Blamey), with the New Zealand Division (Major General Bernard Freyberg) and 6th Australian Division (Major General Sir Iven Mackay). In a few short weeks German intervention completely reversed the Axis fortunes in the area and forced the Allies to evacuate their forces after overrunning both Yugoslavia and Greece, while Rommel had launched an unexpectedly early offensive out of Tripolitania, advanced rapidly through Cyrenaica (capturing Major General Richard O'Connor in the process), laid siege to Tobruk and threatened to press on to the Suez Canal.

In a taste of things to come, two battalions of paratroopers under Oberst Alfred Sturm were used to capture a road bridge over the Corinth Canal, a waterway that ran through a deep gorge dividing the Peloponnese from the Greek mainland, and one of the main escape routes for Allied forces retreating south. The bridge was guarded by a 'close bridge garrison' of British troops and had been set for demolition by the Royal Engineers. The Germans hesitated over launching the operation but once decided, executed it with characteristic speed and flexibility. The British force was adequate for the task of defending the bridge, with a reinforced battalion concentrated on the south side of the bridge supported by AA guns and a few light tanks. There are typically two alternatives in an airborne operation. One is to land the troops some distance from the objectives, avoiding the strongest part of the defences and minimising disruption during the landing itself. This method also allows the paratroopers to form up and assault the objective in good order, and was the procedure adopted for Operation *Market Garden* – the Arnhem assault in 1944. The alternative is to drop the paratroopers as close to their objective as possible in order to maximise surprise and

Allied soldiers of the 5th New Zealand Brigade aboard the *Glengyle* leaving Greece from Porto Rafti in late April 1941. (Alexander Turnbull Library, DA-07493)

New Zealand soldiers from 'W' Force, photographed by N. Blackburn during the retreat through Athens in mid-April 1941 during the Balkan campaign. (Alexander Turnbull Library, DA-10632)

overwhelm the defenders before they can react effectively. This approach does risk greater disruption and heavier casualties while the paratroopers are still vulnerable.

The latter method was chosen for the assault on the Corinth Canal bridge. Early on the morning of 26 April, once the close air support had pounded the defenders, the German vanguard of parachute engineers, loaded in DFS 230 gliders, landed at either end of the bridge. Having seized the bridge they set to work on the demolition charges. They were followed minutes later by some 200 Ju-52 transport aircraft that dropped two battalions of paratroopers, one at each end of the bridge. The paratroopers quickly overwhelmed the defenders after a short but sharp battle. In almost the last act of the battle, a British Bofors gun fired at the engineers on the bridge and actually touched off some disconnected explosives, which seriously damaged the structure. This cut off Allied troops north of the bridge who were subsequently captured, bringing total Allied losses in Greece to over 11,000 men. However, some 18,000 were evacuated to Crete and another 23,000 eventually made their way to Egypt by various means. The Allies lost a large amount of equipment: almost 200 aircraft, over 100 tanks, some 400 artillery pieces, 1,800 machine guns and 8,000 vehicles. Total German casualties in the Yugoslav and Greek campaigns amounted to 11,000. The occupation of these two countries would prove a major commitment in terms of men and matériel needed for the rest of the war. With the Balkan campaign at an end, the countdown started to the only strategic use of airborne forces in history, an operation that would prove to be both the Fallschirmjäger's most glorious achievement and their ultimate downfall.

CHRONOLOGY

1940

28 October Italian forces invade Greece.
23 November Romania joins the Tripartite Pact.
13 December Adolf Hitler issues War Directive No. 20 outlining the planned invasion of Greece, Operation *Marita*. German troops enter Romania.
18 December War Directive No. 21 is issued, concerning the planned attack on the Soviet Union, Operation *Barbarossa*.

1941

1 March Bulgaria joins the Tripartite Pact and German troops prepare to enter the country.
5 March British Expeditionary Force prepares to enter Greece.
25 March Yugoslavia signs the Tripartite Pact.
26 March Anti-royalist coup in Yugoslavia leads to the repudiation of the Tripartite Pact.
27 March War Directive No. 25 is issued outlining Operation *Strafe*, the invasion of Yugoslavia.
6 April Germans launch simultaneous invasions of Yugoslavia and Greece, and the Luftwaffe begins air bombardment of urban targets, including Belgrade.
7 April Operation *Barbarossa* postponed until 22 June. The Metaxas Line broken by German mountain troops.
10 April Axis forces capture Zagreb.
12 April Belgrade falls to German troops.
14 April XVIII Gebirgs Corps penetrates the Mount Olympus defence line and takes Kateríni.
15 April Generalmajor Student submits his plan for the invasion of Crete to Reichsmarschall Göring.
16 April Sarajevo falls to XLVI Panzer Corps.
17 April Churchill gives General Sir Archibald Wavell permission to withdraw 'W' Force from Greece.
18 April German armistice with Yugoslavia comes into effect.
25 April War Directive No. 28 covering the proposed invasion of Crete, Operation *Merkur*, is issued.

BELOW, LEFT **A group of New Zealand troops taking a break in the shade of some trees in a transit area between Hania and Galatos, shortly after they arrived on Crete in late April 1941. They were involved in the final rearguard action before the withdrawal from the island. (Alexander Turnbull Library, DA-01110)**

BELOW, RIGHT **German Gebirgsjäger from Julius Ringel's 5th Gebirgs Division (as given away by the standard German infantry equipment, including the helmet) preparing to board their transports for the journey to Crete, during the early stages of the operation in May 1941. (Alexander Turnbull Library, DA-01313)**

ABOVE, LEFT **A group of Allied soldiers, on the run from the occupying Germans, take cover behind bamboo and oats that were often used for protection in Crete – photographed by Lance Corporal Liddel on 29 July 1941. (Alexander Turnbull Library, DA-03179)**

ABOVE, RIGHT **New Zealand soldiers await evacuation, while keeping under cover from air attack in caves near Sphakion on the south coast on 31 May 1941. (Alexander Turnbull Library, DA-10636)**

26 April German 2nd Fallschirmjäger Regiment assaults bridge over Corinth Canal and captures the town.

27 April Athens falls to German forces.

29 April Kalámai falls, German forces reach the southern coast of Greece.

30 April Allied evacuation ends. Some 25,000 Allied troops have been evacuated to Crete and so Wavell appoints Major General Bernard Freyberg to command the garrison.

1 May The Luftwaffe starts its bombardment of Crete.

16 May 2nd Battalion, the Leicestershire Regiment arrives on board the cruisers of Force 'B' while heavy air attacks occur on Heraklion, Maleme, Souda Bay and Hania.

18 May Air raids continue on Heraklion and Maleme, while HMS *Glengyle* lands the 1st Battalion, Argyll and Sutherland Highlanders (A&SH) at Tymbaki.

OPERATION *MERKUR*

20 May Heavy bombing of Heraklion and Maleme precedes the landing of parachute and glider troops around Maleme (08.00hrs), in Prison Valley (08.15hrs), to the east of Rethymnon (16.15hrs) and around Heraklion (17.30hrs). By nightfall, none of the four main objectives has been taken and the paratroopers have only established a firm perimeter at Maleme.

21 May With pressure building, the New Zealand 22nd Infantry Battalion withdraws, relinquishing Hill 107 to the Germans and thus the airfield. At dawn, the Ju-52 carrying Hauptmann Kleye lands on the western edge of the airfield, confirming the area is free from direct artillery fire. Reinforcements are dropped near Heraklion, Pyrgos and to the west of Maleme airfield, and 100th Gebirgsjäger Regiment starts to arrive (17.00hrs). The Allies start to organise a counterattack, while the Royal Navy intercepts a convoy of Greek vessels carrying elements of 5th Gebirgs Division.

22 May The Allied counterattack manages to reach the eastern edge of Maleme airfield by around 07.30hrs but is forced to withdraw. The Allied position deteriorates and the troops are forced to withdraw to a shorter line, leaving Maleme in German hands. In Prison Valley, around Heraklion and Rethymnon, the paratroopers are too weak to break through the defences. 3rd Fallschirmjäger Regiment in Prison Valley sends out a detachment under Major Heilmann in the hope of linking up with forces moving east from Maleme.

23 May The Germans continue to fly in reinforcements, while Allied forces withdraw to a new line near Galatos, as they are in danger of being outflanked.

24 May Reinforcements are dropped south-west of Heraklion. 85th and 100th Gebirgsjäger Regiments start to probe the Allied frontline around Galatos.

25 May 1st Battalion, A&SH starts arriving at Heraklion only to find their progress blocked. Later that day, the western group of German paratroopers under Major Schultz marches east to join up with the remainder of 1st Fallschirmjäger Regiment. At around dusk a German attack develops towards Galatos. An Allied counterattack only partially restores the situation, and it is decided to withdraw 4th NZ Bde. into reserve and form a new line using 5th NZ Bde. RAF attacks Maleme airfield and destroys some 24 Ju-52s for the loss of seven aircraft.

26 May The Germans break through the Hania–Galatos line and Allied forces withdraw towards Souda Bay. Freyberg decides on a withdrawal to Sphakion so that the troops can be evacuated by sea.

27 May Layforce arrives in Souda Bay. Wavell signals to Churchill that Crete is no longer tenable and the chiefs of staff order the evacuation of the island. A new defence line is formed, nicknamed '42nd Street' just to the west of Souda Bay. The Germans advance, encircling Force Reserve near Hania, but 100th Gebirgsjäger Regiment is stopped in its tracks by an Allied counterattack. Allied forces start to withdraw to Sphakion.

28 May Evacuation starts in earnest with Force 'B' heading for Heraklion and Force 'C' for Sphakion. Italian troops occupy the area of Lasthi.

29 May Some 700 troops embark at Sphakion, while 4,000 are evacuated from Heraklion, although HMS *Imperial* is sunk and Force 'B' is bombed throughout the day. The Allied rearguard continues to carry out an orderly withdrawal, now pursued by 100th Gebirgsjäger Regiment. Germans now control Heraklion and Rethymnon.

30 May Force 'D' from Alexandria embarks over 6,000 men at Sphakion with Force 'C' en route back to Crete. Maleme is bombed again by the RAF. Rearguard is now only a few miles from Sphakion.

31 May Further evacuations are carried out by Force 'C' before dawn with some 1,500 men embarking. Major General Freyberg leaves by Sunderland flying boat while Major General Eric Weston remains in command on Crete.

1 June Force 'D' conducts the final evacuation with 4,000 men embarking at Sphakion. The remaining Allied forces on Crete capitulate with Weston leaving for Egypt on a flying boat.

OPPOSING COMMANDERS

ALLIED COMMANDERS

Major General 'Tiny' Freyberg at over 6ft tall was an imposing man, but is seen here in a relaxed moment. He took over the command of Crete shortly before the invasion on 30 April 1941. (IWM – E3021E)

General Sir Archibald Wavell was appointed as Commander-in-Chief of the newly created Middle East Command on 2 August 1939. Wavell, who was born in 1883 and educated in Winchester, was commissioned into the Black Watch in 1901, serving in both South Africa and India. In 1917 he was sent to represent the Chief of the Imperial General Staff at General Allenby's headquarters during the Egyptian campaign, and later wrote his biography. It was under Wavell's command that O'Connor routed the Italian forces advancing into Egypt in December 1940. One of the major problems Wavell faced was his relationship with the Prime Minister, Winston Churchill, whose complete underestimation of Wavell was made worse by his constantly trying to interfere with his command. He was succeeded by General Claude Auckinleck as C-in-C, Middle East in June 1941 and was posted to the Far East until June 1943 when he was appointed Viceroy of India, a position he held until the end of the war.

Major General Bernard 'Tiny' Freyberg, VC, commanded the Allied garrison on Crete (known as 'Creforce'). Freyberg was one of the war's most charismatic leaders and although born in England, spent all his childhood in New Zealand. In 1914, he came back to Britain and managed to secure a commission, fighting at Gallipoli and on the Western Front. He was wounded a dozen times and received the Victoria Cross at the battle of the Somme. He stayed in the army during the inter-war years, but was finally forced to retire due to ill health.

General Sir Archibald Wavell KCB, CMG, MC, Commander-in-Chief, Middle East, a position he had held since August 1939, lands by boat at Souda Bay to inspect the garrison on 13 November 1940. He faced constant interference with his command from Prime Minister Winston Churchill. (IWM – E1179)

Nevertheless, he offered his services to the New Zealand government in 1939 and, due to his reputation, was given command of the 2nd New Zealand Expeditionary Force. It was the same qualities he had displayed in the First World War, as well as his personal relationship with Winston Churchill, which led to his selection as overall commander of 'Creforce'. After the campaign, he remained the commander of the New Zealand Division through its campaigns in North Africa and Italy and, following the war, became his country's governor general until 1952. In 1953 he was made deputy constable and lieutenant governor of Windsor Castle, taking up residence in the Norman Gateway. He died on 4 July 1963.

Admiral Sir Andrew Browne Cunningham ('ABC'), who had assumed the post of Commander-in-Chief, Mediterranean Station in June 1939, commanded the Royal Navy in the Mediterranean theatre. Born in Dublin in January 1883, Cunningham spent three years at the Naval Preparatory School, Stubbington House and then moved to HMS *Britannia* in 1896. He served with the Naval Brigade as a midshipman during the Boer War and commanded a destroyer, HMS *Scorpion* during the First World War, winning the DSO and two bars. Cunningham's main concern was for the convoys heading for Egypt and the safety of Malta, whose significance he fully appreciated. He adopted an aggressive policy against the Italian fleet, with victories at Calabria, Taranto and Cape Matapan. He was also able to provide valuable support to ground operations, particularly during the campaigns in both Greece and Crete, where the Royal Navy evacuated thousands of Allied troops in the face of powerful opposition from the Luftwaffe.

Brigadier Edward Puttick was in temporary command of the New Zealand Division while Freyberg commanded the island garrison. He was born in Timaru, New Zealand in 1890 and, after joining the Roads Department in 1906, joined the Territorial Force and was commissioned into the 15th (North Auckland) Regiment, later transferring to the 5th (Wellington) Regiment. During the First World War, he served with the New Zealand Rifle Brigade in Egypt, Cyrenaica and on the Western Front, where he rose to command the 3rd Battalion. He took command of the 4th New Zealand (NZ) Brigade in January 1940 until August 1941, becoming Chief of Staff and General Officer Commanding, New Zealand Forces until December 1945.

Brigadier James Hargest was born in Gore, New Zealand in 1891. He fought in the First World War with the Otago Mounted Rifle Regiment, where he commanded the 2nd Battalion and won the Distinguished Service Order and bar, as well as the Military Cross. He became a farmer during the inter-war years and was a Member of the New Zealand Parliament (for the constituency of Invercargill, then Awaura) from 1931. He became CO of the 5th New Zealand Brigade in May 1940. Hargest was killed on 12 August 1944 while attached to the British 50th (Northumbrian) Infantry Division as an observer.

Lieutenant Colonel Howard Kippenberger, commander of the newly formed the 10th New Zealand Brigade, was born in Ladbrooks, New Zealand in 1897 and served as a private soldier with the New Zealand Expeditionary Force during the First World War. He was badly wounded in the arm just after the battle of the Somme by shrapnel and discharged from the army in April 1917. He became a lawyer in Rangiora during the inter-war years and joined the Territorial Force in 1924. He commanded

Colonel Howard Kippenberger (left) and Lieutenant Charles Upham. Kippenberger commanded the 10th New Zealand Brigade on Crete and was awarded the DSO, while Upham won the first of his two Victoria Crosses. (IWM – K1904)

General Claude Auckinleck, who took over the post of Commander-in-Chief, Middle East from Wavell immediately after the Crete campaign, talks to Lieutenant Charles Upham after the award of his Victoria Cross in Egypt. (Alexander Turnbull Library, DA-02165)

the 20th New Zealand Battalion from September 1939 until April 1941, when he took control of the 10th New Zealand Brigade. He assumed command of the 20th New Zealand Battalion again in June 1941 until the end of the year, and then commanded 5th New Zealand Brigade from January 1942 until June 1943 and again from November 1943 until February 1944. He briefly commanded the New Zealand Division (30 April–14 May 1943 and 9 February–2 March 1944) until he was badly wounded after stepping on a mine. After the war, he became the editor-in-chief, *New Zealand War Histories* from 1947 until his death in 1957.

Brigadier Lindsay M. Inglis was born at Mosgiel, Otago, on 16 May 1894, was educated at Waitaki Boys' High School, and studied law at the University of Otago. He also served in the 2nd (South Canterbury) Regiment and joined the New Zealand Expeditionary Force on 30 April 1915 serving with the New Zealand Rifle Brigade. After deploying to Egypt, his battalion was sent to the Western Front in April 1916 and on 15 September 1916 he won the Military Cross. In March 1917 he was transferred to the New Zealand Machine Gun Corps until his discharge in April 1919. He returned to New Zealand and married his fiancée in Wellington in December 1919. Inglis completed his law studies in 1920 and eventually became CO of the 3rd New Zealand Infantry Brigade in July 1931. At the start of the Second World War, Inglis immediately volunteered and took command of the 27th (Machine Gun) Battalion in December 1939 and of the 4th New Zealand Infantry Brigade on Crete on 17 May 1941, immediately before the German invasion. Afterwards, he commanded it throughout the ill-conceived Crusader offensive in late 1941, taking over command of the New Zealand Division at Mersa Matruh after Freyberg was wounded. He also led the division during the attacks on Ruweisat Ridge and the El Mreir depression. He then reorganised the 4th Brigade as an armoured brigade. He briefly served as divisional commander in June/July 1943 in Freyberg's absence, but had little opportunity to command his formation as a whole, as many units were detached to support the infantry brigades. Somewhat disillusioned, he returned to New Zealand and was made a military CBE in 1944. In July 1945 he was appointed president of a military government court in the British zone of occupied Germany and was to preside over criminal cases brought by Germans involving the Allied occupying powers, and cases dealing with Allied nationals.

Brigadier George Alan Vasey commanded the 19th Australian Brigade on Crete, responsible for Georgioupolis and Rethymnon. Born in a suburb of Melbourne on 29 March 1895, he studied at Canterbury Grammar School and Wesley College, and went to the newly opened Royal Military College at Duntroon. He joined the Expeditionary Force in April 1915 and saw action on the Somme, at Messines Ridge, Passchendaele and Amiens. Between the wars he served in India and attended the Quetta Staff College between 1928 and 1929. At the outbreak of the Second World War, he volunteered and became GSO1 (General Staff Officer, Grade 1) for the 6th Australian Division, commanding the 19th Brigade during the Balkan and Crete campaigns. He commanded the 7th Division in the Papua–New Guinea campaign that saw the division advance from Kokoda through Buna to Sanananda during 1942 and in 1943. The unit was airlanded into Markham Valley, capturing Lae and advancing into the Ramu Valley despite stubborn Japanese resistance. He was killed in an air crash in

March 1945 whilst on his way to take command of the 6th Division at Aitipe.

Lieutenant Colonel L.W. Andrew, VC, was commander of the 22nd New Zealand Battalion, defending Maleme and Hill 107. It was his fateful decision to withdraw his battalion, under severe pressure and suffering from poor communications, which handed Maleme airfield to the Germans. He was born in 1897 in Ashurst, New Zealand, and won the Victoria Cross for heroism during the First World War as a corporal in the 2nd Battalion, Wellington Infantry Regiment, New Zealand Expeditionary Force at La Bassee Ville, France, on 31 July 1917. A regular soldier, he commanded the 22nd Battalion from January 1940 until March 1942, but also commanded 5th New Zealand Brigade from 27 November to 8 December 1941. He was Commander, Wellington Area, from November 1943 until December 1946 and then the Central Military District from April 1948 until March 1952.

AXIS COMMANDERS

Alexander Löhr was commander-in-chief of the small Austrian Air Force, and one of the few senior Austrian officers incorporated into the Wehrmacht after the Anschluss of 1936. By the summer of 1939, he was in command of Luftflotte IV, which was one of the two major air formations used in the Polish campaign. Löhr submitted the original plan for an attack on Crete, emphasising the need for a single concentrated drop in the area of Maleme and Hania. After the Crete campaign he supported Von Rundstedt's Army Group South in its drive into the Soviet Union, then became the commander of the Balkan theatre in 1942, air commander in Italy from January to August 1943, and finally commander of the Greek and Aegean area until the end of the war. Löhr was the only Luftwaffe officer, except Kesselring, and the only Austrian except Rendulic, to become a theatre commander. He was an experienced and effective air commander but had very little knowledge of ground operations.

Generalmajor Kurt Student commanded Fliegerkorps XI, assuming control of the new formation in January 1941. The corps included not only the 7th Flieger Division, but also the army's 22nd Luftlande Division, anti-aircraft and medical support units, three wings of Junkers Ju-52 transport aircraft and DFS 230 gliders. Student had started his career as an infantry officer before becoming a fighter pilot in the First World War. During the inter-war years he worked as a gliding instructor, a Reichswehr battalion commander and was head of two Luftwaffe technical departments. In July 1938 he was charged with the formation of the first airborne division, bringing the relevant units under the overall control of the Luftwaffe, as well as being made Inspector of Flying Schools. Student was a man who believed in leading from the front, a characteristic he tried hard to instil in all his subordinate commanders, and it was thus hardly surprising that he was wounded in Holland during the 1940 campaign and awarded the Knight's Cross at its conclusion. Even though the original idea of forming a parachute corps had been Reichsmarschall Hermann Göring's, Student remained the men's spiritual leader through his dedication to hard work and disregard for personal safety. Later in the war he commanded the 1st Parachute Army in Holland, followed by Army Group 'H'. After the war,

A portrait photograph of Generalmajor Kurt Student, commander of Fliegerkorps XI, author of one of the plans to take Crete and founding father of the German airborne forces. (IWM – HU32007)

Generalmajor Julius 'Papa' Ringel commanded the tough 5th Gebirgs Division that was to reinforce the paratroopers once they had captured an airfield. (IWM)

A photograph showing Generalmajor Ringel decorating the Gebirgsjäger of his division after the battle in mid-1941. Ringel displays the *edelweiss* badge of the Gebirgsjäger on his right sleeve. Each man would be given a certificate of authorisation which proved the soldier's right to wear the decoration as German awards were not marked with the recipient's name. (Alexander Turnbull Library, DA-12642)

the Allies put Student on trial for condoning reprisals against civilians on Crete. He was acquitted thanks to the testimony of the 4th New Zealand Brigade commander, Brigadier Inglis, and walked free. He died in 1978 but remains an icon to paratroopers of all nations.

General der Flieger Freiherr (Baron) Wolfram von Richthofen was the commander of Fliegerkorps VIII, which had the mission of supporting Student's Fliegerkorps XI during its campaign on Crete. A cousin of the famous Baron von Richthofen, better known as the 'Red Baron', he himself was a fighter ace during the First World War. He worked in engineering after the Great War and then rejoined the army in 1923, serving for a time as a military attaché in Rome. After transferring to the Luftwaffe, von Richthofen worked in the Air Ministry after 1933 and in 1936 became assistant to the head of the Technical Department. He briefly commanded the 'Kondor' Legion in Spain, which with the campaigns in Poland, the Low Countries and France, helped him perfect the tactical use of close-support aircraft, particularly the Ju-87 Stuka. While sometimes critical of the army, he never let his feelings affect his performance. Göring rated him as one of his best operational commanders, alongside Kesselring. He was promoted to field marshal on 17 February 1943 and was transferred to the Mediterranean theatre from the Eastern Front to try and shore up resistance there.

Generalmajor Eugen Meindl commanded the Luftlande Sturm-regiment that was tasked with capturing and holding Maleme airfield in the first wave of the assault. Meindl had initially been trained as a gunner in the mountain troops and led the 112th Mountain Artillery Regiment during the Norwegian campaign of 1940. Although none of his men had received parachute training, he and some of his gunners were dropped as reinforcements near Narvik. As a result, Meindl became an airborne enthusiast, applied for a transfer to the Fallschirmjäger and passed his training with flying colours. Student recognised his potential and appointed him as the commander of the still embryonic Luftlande Sturmregiment. Unluckily, he was badly wounded very early on in Crete, but went on to command the II Parachute Corps in Normandy after commanding the 'Meindl' Division and the 21st Luftwaffe Field Division on the Eastern Front, playing an important part in the relief of Kholm in 1942.

Generalmajor Julius 'Papa' Ringel, in command of the 5th Gebirgs Division, was born in 1889. He served in the Austrian Army between 1909 and 1938 and was a Nazi before the Anschluss in 1938. He briefly commanded the 3rd Gebirgs Division in 1940 and then transferred to become the commander of the 5th Gebirgs Division as it was being formed in Salzburg during October 1940. The unit would first see action during the Balkan campaign and would be in combat again very soon in Crete. Ringel would go on to command the LXIX Corps in 1944, and then, as General der Gebirgstruppen commanding Korps Ringel, would fight the Russians in southern Austria during 1945.

Oberst Bernard Ramcke and his adjutant Hauptmann Vogel were responsible for helping to train and organise the 5th Gebirgs Division in its airlanding role. He had to take command of the remnants of the Luftlande Sturmregiment at short notice on 21 May after Meindl was seriously wounded. Born in 1889, he joined the navy as a ship's boy but fought in the trenches on the Western Front with the Naval Infantry Division, winning the Iron Cross, First and Second Class, as well as the Prussian Military

Service Cross. After the end of the First World War, he joined one of the most brutal units of the *Freikorps*, General von der Goltz's 'Iron' Division, which terrorised the Baltic States in 1919 on the fringes of the Russian Civil War. He subsequently became an officer in the Reichswehr during the inter-war period. He earned his para-rifleman badge in 1940 at the age of 51 and was awarded the Knight's Cross on 21 August 1941 for his actions during the Crete campaign. Afterwards, he commanded the elite Ramcke Parachute Brigade in the Western Desert, earning his Oakleaves, and then the 2nd Fallschirmjäger Division in Italy. The Oakleaves were followed by the Swords and Diamonds for his defence of Brest in September 1944. He was the 20th out of only 27 members of the German Armed Forces to be awarded the coveted Diamonds.

Commander of the 1st Fallschirmjäger Regiment, Oberst Bruno Bräuer, talking with an Unteroffizier from his regiment during the battle for Heraklion. Bräuer went on to become the most humane of the island commandants. (IWM – MH12797)

Oberst Bruno Bräuer started his military career as an army cadet in 1905 and in 1914 joined a Prussian Infantry Regiment, winning both the Iron Cross, First and Second Class during the First World War. Afterwards he joined the Reichswehr, followed by police group Wecke and took command of the 1st Battalion, General Göring Regiment in 1936. He was appointed commander of the 1st Fallschirmjäger Regiment in 1938, leading it during the campaigns in Poland, France and the Low Countries (receiving a Knight's Cross for the operations in Holland), as well as the Balkans and Crete. After serving in Russia, Bräuer returned to Crete in February 1943 as commandant and eventually commanded the 9th Fallschirmjäger Division in the final stages of the Eastern Front campaign and was captured by the British on 10 May 1945. He was returned to Greece to face trial for alleged war crimes against the local populace and, despite there being very little evidence in that regard, was executed on the sixth anniversary of the battle for Crete. His body was buried in Athens but returned to Crete in the 1970s at the request of the Association of German Airborne Troops.

Oberst Richard Heidrich, formerly a tactics instructor at the military academy in Potsdam, was in command of the 3rd Fallschirmjäger Regiment that landed in Prison Valley on 20 May, tasked with attacking towards Hania and Souda Bay. After consolidating his regiment, Heidrich determined that his force was too weak to force their way to Souda Bay and so waited for the German forces around Maleme to build up and advance eastwards, at which point his regiment joined the attack. Later, he took command of 7th Flieger Division and, after it was renamed 1st Fallschirmjäger Division, commanded it in Italy for the remainder of the war, eventually being captured by a patrol from the 3rd Battalion, the Grenadier Guards. However, while being interrogated by Lieutenant Nigel Nicolson, the intelligence officer, Heidrich almost managed to turn the tables on his captors. He started to talk about the relative merits of Allied and German small arms and, in order to illustrate a point, asked the sentry to pass him his Thompson submachine gun. The guardsman moved to comply, being stopped by Lieutenant Nicolson just in time. Heidrich merely smiled.

Major Walter Koch was in command of the 1st Battalion, Luftlande Sturmregiment, actually the regiment's glider unit. Koch was born in Bonn on 10 September 1910 and after leaving school was commissioned into the police force. In August 1935, however, he transferred to the Luftwaffe, underwent parachute training at Stendal and eventually joined the newly formed 7th Flieger Division. In May 1940 he commanded a battalion-sized unit that stormed the Belgian fortress of Eban Emael, as well as capturing a number of bridges over the Meuse River. As a result, Koch was promoted to major and given the command of the 1st Battalion in the newly expanded Luftlande Sturmregiment in time for Operation *Merkur*. Koch received a serious head wound early on in the battle and played no further part. Having served on the Eastern Front, and with preparations for the invasion of Malta (Operation *Hercules*) cancelled, Koch and the 5th Fallschirmjäger Regiment were deployed to Tunisia in November 1942. It was here at Depienne that Koch managed to intervene to prevent the slaughter of a number of wounded British paratroop POWs. In October 1943, while convalescing in Germany from another head wound received in Tunisia, he was killed in a mysterious car accident while driving in thick fog.

Commander of the 1st Battalion, 3rd Fallschirmjäger Regiment under Heidrich was **Hauptmann Freiherr (Baron) Friedrich August von der Heydte**, born on 30 March 1907 into a Bavarian noble family. He joined the army in April 1925, initially with an infantry regiment but later transferred to the cavalry. Von der Heydte was then released into university life where he studied law at Innsbruck University and joined the Catholic Society, earning the nickname in later years of the 'Rosary Paratrooper'. He also studied at Berlin University and the Austrian Consular Academy. He rejoined his cavalry regiment and with the outbreak of war managed to transfer to the Luftwaffe, joining the 3rd Fallschirmjäger Regiment in August 1940 as a battalion commander. After the campaign in Crete (where he received the Knight's Cross) he served on the Eastern Front, in North Africa and Italy. Heydte was then given command of the 6th Fallschirmjäger Regiment, which he led in Normandy and in the Low Countries. Later in the year he was tasked with raising a paratroop unit to take part in the Ardennes Offensive, where he was taken prisoner, returning to Germany in 1947 to take up university life once more.

Hauptmann Rudolf Witzig commanded No. 9 Kompanie, part of the ill-fated 3rd Battalion, Luftlande Sturmregiment under Major Otto Scherber. Born on 14 August 1916 in Roehlinghausen, he followed the normal educational path for a German boy, but joined the army in April 1935 as a pioneer. He transferred to the army's parachute battalion in August 1938, having developed a keen interest in advanced engineering and airborne assault techniques. The parachute battalion was absorbed into the Luftwaffe and Witzig's engineering skills came to the attention of Hauptmann Walter Koch. The attack was a complete success and Witzig was awarded the Knight's Cross, as well as the Iron Cross, First and Second Class retrospectively. During the invasion of Crete, Witzig was wounded whilst leading an attack on Hill 107 and evacuated by air. This was followed by promotion to major and command of a parachute pioneer battalion in Tunisia, Normandy and on the Eastern Front, eventually gaining command of the 18th Fallschirmjäger Regiment, part of the 6th Fallschirmjäger Division in Holland, where he remained, becoming a POW on 8 May 1945.

OPPOSING FORCES

ALLIED FORCES

The battle for Crete was almost exclusively an infantry affair often fought at very close quarters, with hand-to-hand combat taking place quite frequently. The Allied troops on the island had lost much of their heavier weaponry in the campaign for Greece, and while this did not leave them completely without artillery support, it was, in the main, in the form of anti-aircraft guns and coastal artillery units. This meant the Allies had to aim to defeat an enemy invasion before it gained a foothold, rather than overcoming it in a conventional battle. Nine Matilda 'I' tanks from 'B' Squadron, 7th Royal Tank Regiment were present on the island, but despite being heavily armoured, they had only armour-piercing rounds for their 2-pdr guns, a serious handicap when engaging infantry. There were also the 16 Mk VIB tanks of 'C' Squadron, the King's Own Hussars, armed with machine guns. These had seen heavy service in North Africa and were thus prone to mechanical breakdown. The lack of trucks or Bren gun carriers made it difficult to form a proper mobile reserve.

Almost the only conventional artillery on the island were the 34 Italian 75mm field guns captured by the Greeks, and four 2-pdr anti-tank guns. The anti-aircraft and coastal artillery was also somewhat meagre, with 14 coastal defence guns (3 and 4in.), 20 heavy anti-aircraft guns (3.7in.) and 36 light anti-aircraft guns (40mm).

The German forces were hardly better off, however. The lightly armed airborne troops were supposed to be reinforced by sea, but of the three flotillas conveying most of the artillery and a company from the 5th Panzer Division, the first was badly mauled by the Royal Navy and

A photograph by A.H. Thomas showing a soldier outside the 7th General Hospital, near Galatos, shortly before the German invasion. Despite the large Red Cross symbol, the hospital suffered some damage from air attack during the invasion but treated large numbers of wounded from both sides during the battle. (Alexander Turnbull Library, DA-11712)

the other two aborted. At that point (22 May), the airfield at Maleme was so cratered and littered with wreckage that only a small number of 75mm and 105mm recoilless guns, 37mm and 50mm anti-tank guns and 20mm anti-aircraft guns ever reached the German troops. Where the German forces did have a major advantage over the Allies was the high proportion of automatic weapons that both the paratroopers and mountain troops carried. These weapons, such as the 7.92mm MG34 and 9mm MP40 sub-machine gun, the latter being carried by one in four paratroopers, proved to be very useful in the close-quarter fighting that developed. The majority of men on both sides however, were armed with conventional bolt-action rifles, such as the .303in. Short Magazine Lee Enfield (SMLE) or 7.92mm Mauser Kar98k, which had broadly similar characteristics. These were supplemented by hand grenades and pistols, such as the 9mm Browning, .38 Smith & Wesson and 9mm P08 Luger. The Greek units were in as bad a state, or perhaps even worse, as many of them had lost their personal weapons, as well as their helmets and in some cases even their boots. In any case, their principal small arm was the outdated 6.5mm Mannlicher-Schönauer M1903.

British

By the time of Operation *Merkur*, Great Britain had been at war for some 20 months. Nevertheless, many of the troops on Crete still lacked any combat experience. Although many men had gone to the recruiting offices immediately after Britain's ultimatum to Germany ran out on 3 September 1939, a number had been told to wait for their official call-up papers. Some had gained experience in the fighting in Norway, Belgium, France, as well as North Africa and Greece, and there still existed a cadre of reservists and professional pre-war regulars, particularly among the NCOs. The fact remained, however, that a substantial number of the troops on Crete, including those serving in the infantry, were 'hostilities only' conscripts who had waited with mixed feelings for the papers to land on their doormat. Some of their junior officers were just

A staff officer and some of the 51 nurses from the New Zealand Army Nursing Service with the 1st General Hospital in Souda Bay shortly before their embarkation for Egypt, 29 April 1941. (Alexander Turnbull Library, DA-12253)

as inexperienced, fresh out of Sandhurst and armed with textbook knowledge and a mixture of enthusiasm and apprehension.

Both the world wars were something of an aberration for Britain. For the last two centuries, she had maintained a small but highly professional army designed for colonial warfare and the defence of the empire. Both global conflicts required Britain to rapidly expand her armed forces and fight a continental power with large, capable and well-equipped armed forces that directly threatened the security of the home islands themselves. This expansion meant that for a period of time, the infantry could generally be described as 'enthusiastic amateurs'. This was less applicable to the technical trades, who had the first choice of the better educated conscripts and those with a professional trade, such as mechanical or electrical engineering, who could serve as engineers, signallers, gunners or drivers. The infantry were drawn from every walk of life except the 'reserved' occupations (such as shipyard workers), including clerks and shop assistants, and were often weak and physically unfit as a result of chronic malnutrition and lack of outdoor exercise, a fact highlighted by the Boer War. Psychologically, they were unprepared not only for the confusion of the battlefield, but also for the complex routine of army life, and tended to be contemptuous of both officers and regulations. Beyond that however, they proved remarkably adaptable and by 1945 had been moulded into a formidable fighting force.

The basic fighting unit in most of the armies of this period was the infantry battalion, which in the British case nominally consisted of 22 officers and 757 NCOs and other ranks. It consisted of a headquarters, a support company and four rifle companies, each rifle company including an HQ, three platoons and a support section with Bren guns. Each platoon was made up of an HQ and three sections, each of 10 men. The battalions, part of an infantry regiment in peacetime, were generally amalgamated into three-battalion brigades for operational use; each part of a three-brigade division. There was no British divisional organisational structure on Crete, merely various artillery units, a couple of armoured formations and Brigadier Chappel's 14th Infantry Brigade. This originally consisted of the 2nd Battalion, the York & Lancaster Regiment; 2nd Battalion, the Black Watch; and 1st Battalion, the Welch Regiment. They were joined by the 1st Ranger Battalion (actually the 9th Battalion, King's Royal Rifle Corps) in April and by the 2nd Battalion, the Leicestershire Regiment, and the 1st Battalion, the Argyll & Sutherland Highlanders in May. Unfortunately, Chappel's brigade lacked much of the support usually associated with a formation of this size and was very weak in organic transport, but the troops that were on the island before the Greek campaign were acclimatised, rested and well dug in.

Major General Eric Weston's Mobile Naval Base Defence Organisation (MNBDO) 1, better known later in the war in Burma as 'Viper Force', was a new wartime formation created for the purpose of providing ground defence for naval installations overseas. It consisted of a coastal defence brigade, two anti-aircraft regiments, a searchlight regiment, construction

A photograph showing Lieutenant Roy Farran's destroyed light tank on the outskirts of Galatos, from the book *Gebirgsjäger auf Kreta* by Major Flecker and prepared by Sepp Dobiasch – one of the first published histories of the Crete campaign. (Willhelm Limpert-Verlag, Berlin; 1942). (Alexander Turnbull Library, DA-12645)

engineers and a battalion of infantry. They left Britain in February 1941 but were forced to take the long route via the Cape of Good Hope and Suez Canal as a result of the build-up of the Luftwaffe in the Mediterranean theatre. Due to an administrative error, most of their heavy equipment was offloaded in Palestine instead of Egypt and all Major General Weston could bring to Crete's defence was some 2,000 men and a few extra 4in. coastal guns and 3.7in. anti-aircraft guns. Weston was given temporary command of the island garrison when he flew to Crete in March ahead of his men, but the command was transferred to the more experienced Major General Bernard Freyberg, VC, Commanding Officer of the New Zealand Division, at the end of April.

Australians

Apart from the British, the infantry on the island was drawn from three main contingents – the Australians, New Zealanders and Greeks. The Australians differed from the British in being an all-volunteer force and combat veterans, as well as much better fed, physically fit and used to an outdoor life. While they were even more contemptuous of authority than their British counterparts, often addressing officers as 'mate' rather than 'sir', they were remarkably disciplined in battle. Similarly to Britain, Australia had only a small pre-war regular army, but a very large militia, the Citizen Military Force. Political constraints limited the use of these troops to home defence duties only, but in September 1939 the government called for volunteers to form an Australian Imperial Force to serve overseas. The response was tremendous, and eventually resulted in the creation of the 6th, 7th, 8th and 9th Infantry Divisions and a short-lived 1st Armoured Division. The 2nd AIF (the 1st having been formed during the First World War) began deploying to the Middle East in January 1940, the first formation to move being the 6th Division, commanded by Lieutenant General Sir Thomas Blamey. As a result of the German invasion of the Low Countries in May 1940, the 18th Brigade was diverted to Britain to assist in its defence and eventually became part of the 7th Division instead. The remaining two brigades, the 16th and 17th, were initially modelled on the quad-battalion structure of the First World War, but Blamey remodelled them on the British triangular pattern. The two spare battalions formed the nucleus of a 19th Brigade, which was filled out by another battalion from the 18th Brigade.

Supporting these brigades were the 2/1st, 2/2nd and 2/3rd Field Artillery Regiments, 2/1st Anti-tank Regiment, 2/1st Machine Gun Battalion and 2/1st – 2/3rd Combat Engineer Companies (the '2' representing 2 AIF). Only the 7th Light Battery of the division's anti-aircraft brigade arrived before the campaign started, and so it was an incomplete 6th Australian Division that went to war, first in General O'Connor's triumphant campaign against the Italians in Cyrenaica, and then as part of 'W' Force in Greece. Blamey was then appointed as corps commander and Major General Mackay took command of the division. After the Balkan campaign, just over half of the 14,157 Australians who were evacuated went to Egypt, along with Blamey and Mackay, while the remainder went to Crete, leaving Brigadier Alan Vasey, commander of the 19th Brigade defending the Rethymnon–Georgioupolis sector, as the senior Australian officer.

New Zealanders

The New Zealand infantrymen were in some ways similar to their Australian counterparts, being generally better fed and more physically fit than their British equivalent and used to an outdoor life. They differed in their outlook and psychology to some extent, as New Zealand had never been a penal colony. All however, shared the proud traditions of the ANZAC Corps at Gallipoli during the First World War. As in Australia, there had only been a small standing army in New Zealand prior to the outbreak of war in 1939, but this was backed up by a large militia, known as the Territorial Force. Once again its members were precluded from serving overseas, but here too, the government called for volunteers to form a 2nd New Zealand Expeditionary Force (the 1st again being raised during the First World War). One result was that the New Zealand Division (its correct title) is frequently referred to as the 2nd New Zealand Infantry Division. The New Zealand infantry were highly motivated and although lacking the truculence of the Australians, loathed parade ground 'stiffness' and would on occasion, literally 'go on strike' if they felt they were being treated unfairly. But, like the Australians, once in battle they were superbly disciplined and masters of the bayonet charge, especially the Maoris in Hargest's 5th Brigade.

The expeditionary force began forming in September 1939 and soon consisted of three infantry battalions (18th–20th), which, along with the 4th Artillery Regiment, a company from both the 27th Machine Gun Battalion and 7th Anti-tank Regiment, two companies of engineers and two squadrons of cavalry, formed the 4th Brigade under Brigadier Edward Puttick. Thus elements of the division began deploying to the Middle East in January 1940, but it did not unite as a formation in Egypt until March 1941, still lacking its anti-aircraft regiment. Brigadier James Hargest's 5th Brigade was diverted to Britain, along with the Australian 18th Brigade, and Brigadier A.S. Falconer's 6th Brigade's departure was delayed until August 1940. It arrived just in time for the Greek campaign, and losses during the evacuations to Egypt Freyberg was left with just over 7,000 troops from the division on Crete by the time of Operation *Merkur*. On taking command of the garrison, Freyberg promoted the 4th Brigade's commanding officer, Puttick, to command the division, while Brigadier L.M. Inglis took over 4th Brigade.

Greece

The Second World War started for Greece on 28 October 1940, when it was invaded by the Italians, and ended its first phase with the capitulation to the Germans on 24 April 1941. The Greeks, proud of their hard-won independence from the Turks in the 1820s, have a fierce determination to preserve it. The course of the campaign demonstrated that the Greek

TOP **New Zealand troops from the 6th Brigade aboard the SS *Thurland Castle* during the evacuation of 'W' Force from Greece. The ship, along with the SS *Comliebank*, transferred the brigade from Crete to Egypt on 29 April 1941. (Alexander Turnbull Library, DA-03763)**

ABOVE **Members of the 5th New Zealand Field Regiment having a rest near Wheat Hill after a march while on Crete. These artillerymen acted as infantry during the battle, being part of the 3rd Company, New Zealand Composite Battalion, 10th New Zealand Brigade. (Alexander Turnbull Library, DA-11070)**

A Fallschirmjäger wearing a knee-length camouflage smock, although the majority of those worn in Crete were plain. The large pockets would contain ammunition, maps, message pad, talc, map case and compass. (Alexander Turnbull Library, DA-12631)

soldier was, in general terms, slightly physically and mentally tougher, somewhat better trained, marginally better equipped, much better led and far more motivated than his Italian counterpart. This helps to explain the spectacular reversal of fortunes after the Italian invasion. However, they faced a completely different enemy in the Germans, who were not only better prepared mentally and physically than the Italians, but had far better training, organisation, leadership and equipment.

Greece in the 1930s and 1940s was not a wealthy country and could not afford to maintain its entire 430,000-man army on alert, despite the provocations from Mussolini. Thus it did not begin full mobilisation until after the Italian invasion. The majority of the army moved against the invading forces while some 70,000 men stayed to defend the Metaxas Line in case Bulgaria or Germany initiated a secondary attack. Three battalions of the 5th 'Kríti' Division were left on Crete, along with the 800-strong Gendarmerie and the Heraklion Garrison Battalion. After the Greek surrender, King George II of the Hellenes was evacuated to Crete along with the remnants of the Greek 12th and 20th Infantry Divisions that had continued to fight alongside 'W' Force. No precise figures are available for the number of men that were reorganised, alongside the existing infantry battalions, into a number of 'regiments' by a British liaison officer, Colonel Guy Salisbury-Jones, but they numbered somewhere in the region of 9,000 troops.

The Royal Navy

The Royal Navy was both feared by the Italians and respected by the Germans who had very few naval forces of their own in the Mediterranean. Following the fall of France, the Admiralty reorganised and reinforced its forces in the theatre into eastern and western fleets based in Alexandria and Gibraltar respectively, the boundary between the two being the strategically important island of Malta. By May 1941, Admiral Cunningham's eastern Mediterranean fleet had already been depleted by the loss of two destroyers during the evacuation of 'W' Force from Greece, but this was merely a taste of what was to come. Cunningham reported that his ships had expended almost half their anti-aircraft ammunition and that with the available stocks would only be able to replenish them to three quarters capacity. The Luftwaffe's Fliegerkorps VIII was now operational from airfields in southern Greece and daylight naval operations were increasingly hazardous, especially during Operation *Merkur*, due to the lack of friendly air cover. The last of the RAF's fighters had been evacuated the day before the invasion began and attrition of the aircraft from the carrier HMS *Formidable* soon undermined their effectiveness. During the battle and the evacuation, Cunningham lost three cruisers and another six destroyers, with three battleships, *Formidable*, six cruisers and seven destroyers damaged. The only consolation was that the German reinforcement convoys were turned back and some 17,000 Allied servicemen were evacuated.

AXIS FORCES

Fallschirmjäger

The men of the 7th Flieger Division who spearheaded the assault on Crete were all volunteers. Professionals, tough, physically fit, well trained and with excellent officers at every level, they were highly disciplined and motivated and encouraged to use their initiative whenever possible. They rightly considered themselves an elite corps and the majority were now combat veterans from the campaigns in Norway, Holland, Belgium, France and Greece. While conscription was largely loathed in Britain, it was actually welcomed in Germany as signifying the end of the restrictions of the hated Versailles Treaty, signed at the end of the First World War. Loyalty to the Nazi regime amongst the younger generation had been encouraged by a steady stream of Nazi propaganda and many had served in the paramilitary Hitler Youth. Even in the dark inter-war years, the German armed forces had maintained a cadre of high-quality officers and NCOs. This allowed the military to expand rapidly once the terms of the Versailles Treaty had been repudiated. In the early years of the war, before the pernicious effects of the horrific losses on the Eastern Front were felt, the standard of German training, discipline and morale in the armed forces was first rate.

The call for volunteers to form the first Fallschirmjäger battalion had gone out in 1936 with a paratrooper training school established at Stendal-Bostel airfield outside Berlin. The CO of the new battalion was a certain Bruno Bräuer. By the outbreak of war, having consolidated control of the parachute, glider and air transport forces, the Luftwaffe had enough men to form the nucleus of an airborne division under the command of Generalmajor Kurt Student, based at Tempelhof airfield, near Berlin. By 1941, it had grown into a full division, commanded by Generalleutnant Willhelm Süssmann, consisting of three parachute regiments (Fallschirmjäger Regiment 1, 2 and 3 under the command of Bräuer, Sturm and Heidrich) and a semi-autonomous air assault regiment (Luftlande Sturmregiment under the command of Generalmajor Eugen Meindl), supported by artillery, anti-tank, machine gun and combat engineer battalions. The three parachute regiments had three parachute battalions apiece, while the air assault regiment had three parachute battalions and a glider battalion (under the command of Major Walter Koch). The strength of each parachute battalion averaged around 700 men and comprised three infantry companies, a head-quarters company, a support company and a signals section. The entire battalion, along with all its heavy equipment including radios, heavy weapons, ammunition, medical supplies and rations, was airdropped. The equipment was dropped in lightweight con-tainers. Neither the paratroopers nor the containers could be controlled while they descended, as the majority of parachutes used were still the older RZ16 that lacked the lift webs or 'risers' of American and British designs.

A group of German mountain troops from the 5th Gebirgs Division line up for a photograph while waiting to embark on their Ju-52 transport aircraft, which will take them to Maleme airfield. Their faces betray something of the nervousness they must have felt as the Gebirgsjäger were being airlifted into battle for the first time. (Alexander Turnbull Library, DA-01315)

A paratrooper takes a swig of his water bottle as his squad prepares to move on. In this regard he is lucky as the hot climate made water a precious commodity, especially for the paratroopers who had been cut off from regular supply around Heraklion and Rethymnon. (B.L. Davis Collection)

A group of German troops including Fallschirmjäger and men of the motorcycle battalion, part of the 5th Gebirgs Division. These troops are probably from the 95th Motor Cycle Battalion, which formed part of the Wittmann Advanced Guard, tasked with the initial pursuit of the Allied forces to the east and relieving the paratroopers around Heraklion and Rethymnon. (B.L. Davis Collection)

Two paratroopers greet each other, providing an excellent close up of their personal equipment. The Allied troops were impressed with the lavish scale of equipment carried by German paratroopers. Also, given the high casualty rate on Crete, finding a familiar face would have been a welcome sight indeed. (B.L. Davis Collection)

5th Gebirgs Division

Instead of the 22nd Luftlande Division (which was guarding the Ploesti oilfields in Romania), the paratroopers would be reinforced by the 5th Gebirgs Division under the command of Generalmajor Julius 'Papa' Ringel. The majority of troops in this division were volunteers and had combat experience, having come from a number of other divisions that had seen service in the Low Countries and Norway before the 5th had started forming in Salzburg in October 1940. The majority of the soldiers were recruited from Austria and the alpine region of southern Germany and were tough, physically fit and highly motivated.

The division was organised along similar lines to a conventional infantry division, although it had only two rifle regiments (85th and 100th Gebirgsjäger Regiments), each with three battalions, and the 95th Gebirgsartillerie Regiment with two artillery battalions along with signals, reconnaissance, anti-tank and engineer battalions. With just under 14,000 men, it was weaker in manpower than a standard infantry division. However, for the Crete campaign, it was reinforced with the 141st Gebirgsjäger Regiment from the 6th Gebirgs Division. Each battalion had the usual three rifle companies, headquarters company and support elements. Neither Ringel nor his men expected their sudden transfer to Student's Fliegerkorps XI as none of them had any experience in airborne warfare, but their contribution to the outcome of the battle cannot be underestimated.

Fliegerkorps VIII

Despite the fact that a large share of the credit can be given to Student's Fliegerkorps XI for victory in the campaign on Crete, some credit is due to the airmen of the other main component of Luftflotte IV, Fliegerkorps VIII, commanded by General Freiherr Wolfram von Richthofen. They proved highly effective in wearing down Allied ground forces and limiting the impact of the Royal Navy on Allied operations. Fliegerkorps VIII comprised seven Geschwader, the equivalent of an RAF Group. Three of these were equipped with Ju-87R Stuka dive bombers (Sturzkampfgeschwader 1, 2 and 77), one with Dornier Do-17Z twin-engine bombers (Kampfgeschwader 2), one with a mixture of Ju-88A and Heinkel He-111H twin engine bombers (Lehrgeschwader 1), one with Messerschmit Bf 110C and D twin-engine fighter-bombers (Zerstörergeschwader 26) and one with Messerschmidt Bf 109E single-seat fighters (Jagdgeschwader 77). In addition, Luftflotte IV contained reconnaissance and air-sea rescue units that saved many lives after the Royal Navy intercepted the first of the reinforcement convoys. Fliegerkorps XI itself could also deploy three Geschwader of Junkers Ju-52/3 transports (KGzbV 1–3) and an airlanding group of DFS 230 gliders. It must be remembered that coming so soon after the Balkan campaign, a large number of aircraft were awaiting servicing and a number of aircrew had been killed or injured, limiting the number of aircraft available for Operation *Merkur*.

OPPOSING PLANS

AXIS PLANS

With the issuing of War Directive No. 25, preparations for the invasion of Crete could begin, but it took time to assemble the necessary men and equipment, scattered as they were all across Europe. As a result, D-Day for Operation *Merkur* was put back until 20 May, enabling the confused defence of Crete to be put into some sort of order. Logistics also dominated the considerations of the targets to attack, as an airborne attack usually relies on surprise, speed and rapid reinforcement. As the first of these factors had already been compromised, the planners looked at the extent to which they could capitalise on the other two. During the early planning process General der Flieger Alexander Löhr (Commander, Luftflotte IV) favoured a single concentrated drop to seize the airfield at Maleme, followed by a build-up of additional infantry and heavy weapons, and then a conventional advance up the island from west to east. Such an approach however, might allow the British time to reinforce the garrison either by sea, or by landing troops at either Heraklion or Rethymnon. This could allow them to sustain a defence of the island. Concerned at this prospect and by the slow build-up that would result from the seizure of a single airfield, Generalmajor Kurt Student (Commander, Fliegerkorps XI) suggested no less than seven separate drops, the most important being around the airfields at Maleme, Rethymnon and Heraklion, with the focus on Heraklion. Student's plan would enable the Germans to seize all the main strategic points at the outset, so long as resistance on the ground was minimal.

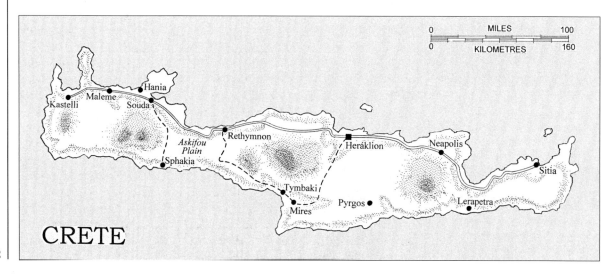

General Wavell stops to talk to an officer while inspecting a 3.7in. anti-aircraft gun position, a number of which were targets for the glider landings on the first day by the Genz and Altmann detachments. Richthofen's Fliegerkorps VIII only lost some 30 aircraft during the battle so their effectiveness against low-flying targets is open to question. (IWM – E1188)

All the planners (including the Kriegsmarine's Konteradmiral Karl-Georg Schuster) agreed, however, that Maleme should be one of the main targets. It was closest to the island's administrative centre, Hania, and Souda Bay, and to the Greek mainland. The latter was important as the 502 operational Ju-52s could not carry all the assault elements in a single drop; the maximum was around 6,000 in one lift. This meant that, even had German intelligence estimates proved correct, the attacking forces would have been at a 1:2 disadvantage. The only answer was to turn the Ju-52s around as quickly as possible to allow a second lift on D-Day. As a back-up the Germans could send a proportion of the assault force by sea, to exploit the foothold gained by the paratroopers. Maleme, being the closest airfield to the mainland, would shorten the time the troopships would be at sea and reduce their vulnerability to interception by the Royal Navy. Finally, Maleme's close proximity to the mainland would allow even Messerschmitt Bf 109 fighters fitted with bomb racks a reasonable amount of flying time over the island, enhancing the potency of available air support.

In the end, Göring imposed a compromise solution between these two different approaches. The drops on D-Day would now be made in two waves: the first in the morning around Hania and the airfield at Maleme, the second in the late afternoon against the airfields at Heraklion and Rethymnon. This would be followed on D+1 by the arrival of the mountain troops of 5th Gebirgs Division under Generalmajor Julius Ringel and the seaborne elements. The assault force on the first day would be split into three groups:

Gruppe West, commanded by Generalmajor Eugen Meindl, consisted of the entire Luftlande Sturmregiment (minus two companies of glider troops that were to be attached to Gruppe Mitte), which would land in the first wave and had the objective of securing Maleme airfield.

Gruppe Mitte, under the divisional commander, Generalleutnant Willhelm Süssmann, the first wave would consist of the divisional headquarters along with the two glider companies from the Luftlande Sturmregiment as well as Oberst Richard Heidrich's 3rd Fallschirmjäger Regiment, reinforced by engineer and AA units. Their objective would be to land in Prison Valley and attack towards Hania and Souda. The second wave would be commanded by Oberst Alfred Sturm and consist of the 1st and 3rd Battalions, 2nd Fallschirmjäger Regiment, with the town of Rethymnon as its objective.

Gruppe Ost, commanded by Oberst Bruno Bräuer and landing in the second wave, consisted of the 1st Fallschirmjäger Regiment, reinforced by the 2nd Battalion, 2nd Fallschirmjäger Regiment (FJR) with Heraklion as its objective.

ALLIED PLANS

German intelligence had badly underestimated the Allied strength on the island. The defence of Greece and Crete was one of the many operations General Sir Archibald Wavell (Commander-in-Chief, Commonwealth Forces Middle East) had been forced to undertake with inadequate resources all around his theatre. There were acute shortages of aircraft, heavy artillery, armoured vehicles and even basic supplies that made his job even more problematic, a situation exacerbated by the losses suffered during the evacuation from Greece, including much of the infantry's organic heavy weapons. In addition many units were now disorganised, and their morale had taken a hard knock. There was no properly functioning radio net and communications proved to be almost non-existent. Nevertheless, the forces on the island numbered some 32,000 Commonwealth troops and 10,000 Greek soldiers, significantly more than the German intelligence estimate of some 10,000 Commonwealth troops and the remnants of ten Greek divisions.

On Crete itself, Freyberg identified five main objectives to defend: the airfields at Maleme, Rethymnon, Heraklion, the administrative centre of Hania and the port at Souda. While his assessments of the nature of the coming assault, its timing and targets was generally good, Freyberg's options were limited. Due to the security restrictions surrounding the decoded transcripts of German 'Enigma' transmissions, it was difficult for him to be confident of the quality of the intelligence he received. The garrison, as well as suffering from poor communications and a lack of

Soldiers Cyril Ericson (holding the map case) and Ernie Avon standing by some discarded German parachutes amongst olive trees near Galatos. Trees and rough ground were always a hazard for parachutists. (Alexander Turnbull Library, DA-00470)

TOP **Allied troops in a transit camp, near Souda Bay on the island of Crete, just before the invasion. Transit camps were set up at regular intervals along main transportation routes, to house troops that were moving from one position to another as the shortage of transportation meant that in many instances, a unit would have to move in shifts. (Alexander Turnbull Library, DA-01040)**

ABOVE **A life-jacketed Gebirgsjäger looks out over the side of one of the Greek fishing boats in the 1st Motor Sailing Flotilla towards the Italian destroyer, the *Lupo*. The convoy was intercepted by the Royal Navy on the night of the 21/22 May 1941 and mostly sunk. (Alexander Turnbull Library, DA-01308)**

heavy weapons, was also handicapped by a chronic shortage of motor transport. There was little prospect of effective air cover and no-one was sure if the Royal Navy could intervene in any meaningful way in the event of a seaborne threat. Freyberg was thus forced to organise his forces into groups of roughly equal strength, split between the objectives, with a strong eye to defending against a seaborne invasion, as well as the threat from the air.

The New Zealand Division was deployed around the Maleme–Galatos area, under the watchful eye of 'Creforce' Headquarters near Hania, and consisted of the 4th Brigade under Brigadier Inglis (18th, 19th and 20th New Zealand Infantry Battalions), the 5th Brigade under Brigadier Hargest (21st, 22nd, 23rd New Zealand and 28th (Maori) Infantry Battalions) and a new 10th Brigade under Colonel Howard Kippenberger (New Zealand Divisional Cavalry Detachment and the Composite Battalion), as Brigadier Falconer's 6th Brigade had been sent to Egypt.

Major General Eric Weston commanded the Mobile Naval Base Defence Organisation (MNBDO) 1 that was concentrated around Souda and reinforced by two composite Australian battalions, named after their parent organisations (16th and 17th Brigades) and the 2/2 Field Artillery Regiment acting as infantry.

1st Battalion, the Welch Regiment (from 14th Brigade), along with the 1st Ranger Battalion (9th Battalion, King's Royal Rifle Corps) and Northumberland Hussars formed a reserve near Hania.

Brigadier Vasey's reinforced 19th Australian Brigade, consisting primarily of 2/1st, 2/7th, 2/8th and 2/11th Infantry Battalions, three batteries from the 2/3rd Field Regiment, some engineers and machine gun troops, was deployed around Rethymnon and Georgioupolis.

Brigadier Chappel's 14th Brigade defended Heraklion and consisted of: 2nd Battalion, the Leicestershire Regiment; 2nd Battalion, the York and Lancashire Regiment; 2nd Battalion, the Black Watch; 1st Battalion, the Argyll and Sutherland Highlanders (who were still at Tymbaki when the invasion took place) and the Australian 2/4th Infantry Battalion (from 19th Brigade).

Finally, the Greek forces were divided as follows: the 1st, 6th and 8th Regiments in the Maleme–Galatos area; the 2nd Regiment in the Souda–Hania area; the 4th and 5th Regiments along with the Gendarmerie were stationed in the Rethymnon–Georgioupolis area; while the 3rd and 7th Regiments and the Garrison Battalion were deployed around Heraklion. Despite misgivings about their performance from many Allied officers, the Greeks would put up a stubborn fight, helped by the acquisition of weapons from dead paratroopers and the occasional weapons container.

In fact, the British picture of German intentions was far better than the German information on Allied dispositions. From the end of April, a stream of 'Ultra' intelligence, decrypted by the code-breaking office at Bletchley Park, indicated that the Germans were very near to launching an all-out airborne invasion of Crete with the emphasis being on the capture of the airfields, and then following that up with air transport of reinforcements, with some coming by sea. Additionally, it was very difficult for Löhr to conceal the build-up of Luftflotte IV in Greece. This information was passed along to Freyberg, but its impact was diluted to protect the secret of the 'Ultra' breakthrough. Freyberg was told that the information had come from 'highly placed spies in Athens'. In fact, 'Ultra' proved to be something of a double-edged sword in that the information coming from the German 'Enigma' transmissions was, in the main, pretty reliable, but it was not always complete and the analysts at Bletchley Park often made mistakes in trying to fill in the gaps. In this case they believed that 5th Gebirgs Division had been attached to Fliegerkorps XI in addition to the 22nd Luftlande (Air Landing) Division, rather than replacing it, and that the Italian Navy would provide proper support so that the seaborne force would be proportionately larger and the greater threat. As a result it was the seaborne threat, rather than the airborne one, that caused Freyberg the greatest worry.

Further confirmation came when a German Bf 110 crashed in Souda Bay. It was found to contain the map case and operational order for the 3rd Fallschirmjäger Regiment, and a summary of the whole operation. The Greeks made the discovery and, unfortunately, despite the fact that it confirmed their own intelligence, the British command decided it was a ruse. Furthermore, it did not fit in with preconceived British ideas, and thus Freyberg continued to concentrate on the seaborne element of the operation with his units spread along the coast. The Allies failed either to concentrate their defence around the airfields or to put them beyond use; the RAF, convinced it would eventually return in strength, prevented the latter. There was also only a small Allied reserve in the event that the Germans captured an airfield. The scene was set therefore for one of the most daring uses of airborne troops in history, the German attackers with a dreadfully inadequate picture of their target and enemy, the Allies effectively looking in the wrong direction.

TOP **A group of Junkers Ju-52 transports from KGzbV 1 under Oberst Morzik on Megara airfield, waiting for the invasion of Crete to begin in mid-May 1941. 533 Ju-52s were used in the Crete campaign, a large proportion of the Luftwaffe's inventory, of which they suffered almost 200 lost in action. (Alexander Turnbull Library, DA-01310)**

ABOVE **Members of the 28th (Maori) Battalion on the wharf in Alexandria immediately after their arrival from Crete. They were evacuated from Sphakion on 30 May 1941 after performing well throughout the campaign. (Alexander Turnbull Library, DA-09662)**

THE ASSAULT ON CRETE

On the morning of 20 May 1941, D-Day for the German invasion of Crete, the sun rose into a clear sky with very little breeze, promising a hot, early summer's day. Even before dawn, however, at Greek airfields such as Megara, Corinth and Tanagra, the Ju-52s from Fliegerkorps XI, with their paratroopers aboard, fired up their engines and started to taxi for take-off. There were problems immediately as the first few transports left huge clouds of dust on the dry, unmetalled runways. It took time for the dust to settle, playing havoc with the carefully planned timetable. Eventually however, the Ju-52s formed up and then headed for their objectives. Unfortunately, one of the first German casualties was Generalleutnant Willhelm Süssmann, commanding officer of the 7th Flieger Division, who was aboard a glider that cut across the slipstream of a Heinkel He-111. The glider separated from its towrope and crashed on the island of Aegina, killing the occupants. Süssmann was due to drop as part of the first wave, with his divisional headquarters landing alongside 3rd Fallschirmjäger Regiment in Prison Valley.

MALEME, 20 MAY

Before the main body of the first wave had reached the coast of Crete, Fliegerkorps VIII had started to soften up the defences of the island, and the glider companies of the Luftlande Sturmregiment that were to support Gruppe West had started to land around 08.00hrs. The initial

German paratroopers from the 3rd Fallschirmjäger Regiment slowly drifting to the ground, near Galatos on 20 May 1941. Many of the paratroopers who landed in this area made their way southeast to find the main body of their regiment. (Alexander Turnbull Library, DA-11975)

MALEME

20–22 May 1941, viewed from the northeast showing the initial German landings and attempts to secure the airfield, the confused Allied response and the disjointed attempts to counterattack.

Note: Gridlines are shown at intervals of ½ mile/0.8km

ALLIED FORCES

A HQ, 5th New Zealand Brigade – Brig J. Hargest
B HQ, 22nd New Zealand Infantry Battalion – LtCol L.W. Andrew
C HQ, Company – Lt G.G. Beaven
D A Company – Maj S. Hanton
E B Company – Capt. K.R.S Crarer
F C Company – Capt S.H. Johnson
G D Company – Capt T.C. Campbell
H 21st New Zealand Infantry Battalion – LtCol J.M. Allen
I 23rd New Zealand Infantry Battalion – LtCol D.F. Leckie
J Field Punishment Centre – Lt W.J.G. Roach
K 19 Army Troops Company – Capt J.N. Anderson
L New Zealand Engineer Detachment (7 Field Company) – Capt J.B. Ferguson
M 28th (Maori) Infantry Battalion – LtCol G. Dittmer
N 20th New Zealand Infantry Battalion – Maj J.T. Burrows
O One troop from 3rd Hussars – Lt R.A.Farran
P 22nd New Zealand Infantry Battalion (22 May)

GERMAN FORCES

1 HQ, Luftlande Sturmregiment – Generalmajor E. Meindl
2 2nd Battalion, Luftlande Sturmregiment – Maj E. Stentzler
3 4th Battalion, Luftlande Sturmregiment – Hauptmann W. Gericke
4 HQ, 1st Battalion, Luftlande Sturmregiment – Maj W.Koch
5 1st Glider Detachment, 3rd Company, 1st Battalion – Oblt W. von Plessen
6 2nd Glider Detachment (elements), 4th Company, 1st Battalion– Maj W. Koch
7 3rd Glider Detachment – Maj F. Braun
8 9th Company (elements), 3rd Battalion – Hauptmann R. Witzig
9 10th Company, 3rd Battalion – Oblt Schulte-Sasse
10 11th Company (elements), 3rd Battalion – Oblt Jung
11 12th Company, 3rd Battalion – Oblt Gansewig
12 16th Company, 4th Battalion – Oblt Hoefeld
13 Ad hoc groups of Fallschirmjäger

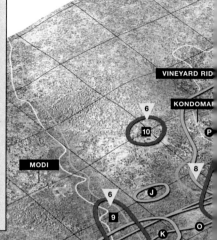

VINEYARD RID

KONDOMA

MODI

PLATANIAS

N

5th NZ x 2nd NZ

HARGEST

▼ EVENTS

1. **08.00HRS ONWARDS, 20 MAY. Parachute and glider landings by the Luftlande Sturmregiment begin. Von Plessen and Braun are killed, their detachments managing to seize the bridge over the Tavronitis River and establish a bridgehead in the RAF camp.**

2. **Major Koch is seriously wounded and his detachment scattered.**

3. **2nd and 4th Bns., LLSR land in good order just west of the Tavronitis.**

4. **16th Company lands to the south near Polemarhi.**

5. **Meindl sends 5th and 7th Companies from 2nd Bn. under Major Stentzler to take Hill 107 from the south. Meindl is then badly wounded in the chest.**

6. **3rd Bn. is badly scattered to the south and east of the airfield and suffers heavy casualties.**

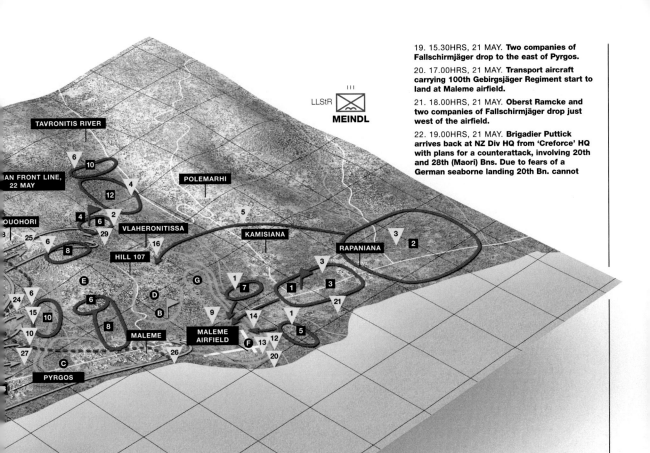

19. 15.30HRS, 21 MAY. **Two companies of Fallschirmjäger drop to the east of Pyrgos.**

20. 17.00HRS, 21 MAY. **Transport aircraft carrying 100th Gebirgsjäger Regiment start to land at Maleme airfield.**

21. 18.00HRS, 21 MAY. **Oberst Ramcke and two companies of Fallschirmjäger drop just west of the airfield.**

22. 19.00HRS, 21 MAY. **Brigadier Puttick arrives back at NZ Div HQ from 'Creforce' HQ with plans for a counterattack, involving 20th and 28th (Maori) Bns. Due to fears of a German seaborne landing 20th Bn. cannot**

move until relieved by Australian 2/7 Bn. 20.10hrs, 21 May. NZ Division HQ orders forces to concentrate for a counterattack.

23. 02.45HRS, 22 MAY. **20th Bn. starts arriving, C and D Coys first, due to the fragmented arrival of the Australian 2/7 Bn. from Georgioupolis to relieve 20th Bn. Major Burrows leaves orders that the remainder of the battalion is to follow and join the attack as they are relieved.**

24. 03.00HRS, 22 MAY. **23rd Bn. conducts a local attack to keep the Germans off balance, while the main counterattack starts at 03.30hrs. As it progresses, the force has to fight a series of separate actions that delay progress and cause disorganisation. At dawn the force is still well short of the airfield and starts to receive the attention of the Luftwaffe.**

25. 07.00HRS, 22 MAY. **21st Bn. starts an attack on LtCol Allen's own initiative.**

26. 07.30–08.00HRS, 22 MAY. **Elements of D, B and A Coys, 20th Bn., reach the eastern edge of the airfield but resistance is heavy. With the battalion badly disorganised, Major Burrows orders a withdrawal.**

27. 08.00HRS, 22 MAY. **By this time C Coy, 20th Bn. is engaged in fierce fighting in Pyrgos and the troop from the 3rd Hussars is bogged down just outside the town. Having consolidated with its B Coy, 28th (Maori) Bn., in conjunction with A Coy, 23rd Bn., advances to a point just south of Pyrgos.**

28. 08.30HRS, 22 MAY. **HQ Coy, 21st Bn., reaches Xamouohori.**

29. 10.30HRS, 22 MAY. **A and B Coys, 21st Bn. reach a position near Vlaheronitissa, but despite reinforcement cannot make further progress. A German counterattack in the afternoon forces all three Coys to retire (around 15.15hrs). They meet LtCol Allen just after 15.30hrs.**

12. DAWN, 21 MAY. **A Ju-52 transport aircraft carrying Hauptmann Kleye lands on the western edge of the airfield, confirming that this area is not under direct artillery fire.**

13. 08.00HRS, 21 MAY. **Six Ju-52s land with supplies and ammunition. Another lands soon after to evacuate some of the badly wounded including Meindl.**

14. MORNING, 21 MAY. **Gericke consolidates 4th Bn. and Regimental Headquarters with the Von Plessen and Braun detachments and continues to press east towards the airfield.**

15. MORNING, 21 MAY. **With pressure building up from the west and south, the disintegration of communications, losses incurred in the counterattack and the failure of B Coy, 28th Bn. to appear, 22nd Bn. withdraws.**

16. MORNING, 21 MAY. **5th and 7th Companies push towards Hill 107, only to find the Allied positions abandoned. They secure the positions with survivors from the other groups.**

17. 11.15HRS, 21 MAY. **Hargest requests reinforcements from NZ Division HQ to conduct a counterattack towards Maleme airfield.**

18. AFTERNOON, 21 MAY. **Freyberg signals Wavell that the main danger is in the Maleme sector.**

7. 17.00HRS, 20 MAY. **A request to Brig Hargest from LtCol Andrew (CO 22nd Bn.) for 23rd Bn. to counterattack is refused as 21st and 23rd Bns. are already in action with Fallschirmjäger landing all around the three forward battalions.**

8. Both 21st and 23rd Bn. beat off the initial attacks and then adopt a posture of aggressive patrolling.

9. 17.15HRS, 20 MAY. **A local counterattack begins towards the bridge over the Tavronitis by 14th Platoon, C Coy, 22nd Bn. supported by two tanks. The attack fails.**

10. DUSK, 20 MAY. **A Coy, 23rd Bn. under Capt Watson moves off to reinforce 22nd Bn., reaching its positions around 22.00hrs.**

11. 19.00HRS, 20 MAY. **B Coy, 28th (Maori) Bn. under Capt Royal leaves to reinforce 22nd Bn.**

A Ju-52 goes down in flames after being hit by anti-aircraft fire over Heraklion airfield on 20 May 1941. It can be seen that a number of paratroopers, probably from the 1st Fallschirmjäger Regiment have still managed to jump from it. While the Ju-52 was quite vulnerable to anti-aircraft fire (as are all transports at the moment they are dropping paratroopers) the majority of losses occurred at Maleme. (IWM – A4144)

The same Ju-52 crashes near to Heraklion airfield during the German invasion Crete. Another aircraft continues to drop paratroopers. The 1st Fallschirmjäger Regiment, reinforced with a battalion from the 2nd Fallschirmjäger Regiment dropped around Heraklion. The 2nd Battalion, 1st Fallschirmjäger Regiment suffered heavy casualties as it landed east and west of the airfield. (Alexander Turnbull Library, PAColl-5547-007)

glider landings just to the west of Maleme proved relatively successful and the paratroopers from Oberleutnant Wulf von Plessen's detachment (3rd Company) and part of the regimental headquarters detachment under Major Franz Braun, managed to land in the river bed, capture the bridge over the Tavronitis, knock out the anti-aircraft positions and secure a bridgehead on the western outskirts of the airfield, despite both commanders being killed. The 4th Company under Hauptmann Kurt Sarrazin and the battalion headquarters with Major Walter Koch came down around Hill 107, defended by A and B Companies of the 22nd New Zealand Infantry Battalion under Major S. Hanton and Captain K. Crarer respectively. The paratroopers suffered heavy casualties with Sarrazin killed and Koch wounded in the head soon after landing; the survivors were scattered across the hillside.

The 3rd Battalion, under Major Otto Scherber, started dropping at this point and landed right on top of the New Zealand defensive positions just south of the coast road. The 9th (Witzig), 11th (Jung) and 12th (Gansewig) Companies came down on top of parts of the 21st, 22nd and 23rd New Zealand Infantry Battalions, and the 10th Company (Schulte-Sasse) landed very near to the Field Punishment Centre and New Zealand Engineer Group. The battalion suffered very badly as a result, some being killed as they dropped[1] and many being killed as they searched for weapons containers. Small groups of survivors did form quickly, however, and set about locating isolated defensive positions where they could either carry out hit-and-run attacks or wait for relief.

1 Tests done later in the war refuted Allied claims to have killed many Fallschirmjäger while they descended. It took an average of 340 rounds by a trained marksman to achieve a hit at 150m – it rose to 1,708 rounds at twice that distance.

TOP **German paratroopers dropping from Ju-52s transport aircraft during the first hours of the invasion. This sight would have greeted many of the Allied troops defending Crete on that first day. The Ju-52 carried three crew and up to 17 airlanding troops, or 13 paratroopers, as well as up to four equipment containers with the static lines attached to the bomb shackles or underwing racks. (IWM – E3265E)**

ABOVE **A crashed German DFS 230 glider on Crete, possibly from the 4th Company of Walter Koch's 1st Battalion, Luftlande Sturmregiment near to Hill 107, 20 May 1941. Two of the occupants lie dead on the ground nearby, indicating that they were under fire from the moment they touched down. (Alexander Turnbull Library, DA-01156)**

Meanwhile, the 4th Battalion under Hauptmann Walther Gericke, along with part of the regimental headquarters, landed west of the Tavronitis, minus the 16th Company under Oberleutnant Höfeld, which landed further south to act as a flank guard. The 2nd Battalion under Major Edgar Stentzler landed east of Spilia, while a platoon under Leutnant Peter Mürbe landed away to the west with the intention of capturing the unfinished airfield near Kastelli. Both formations had a much easier time of it than their comrades as they were further away from the New Zealand defensive positions and hidden by the dust clouds kicked up by continued Luftwaffe ground support and the landing of the glider troops. They managed to land and form up relatively intact. Meindl, realising that things had gone awry with the landings, especially those of the 3rd Battalion, collected the forces at his disposal around his HQ and dug in on the airfield's perimeter and ordered Stentzler to take the 5th (Herterich) and 7th (Barmetler) Companies from his battalion and capture Hill 107, the key to Maleme airfield, with a long sweeping flank march to the south. Soon after this both Meindl and his adjutant, Oberleutnant von Seelen, were wounded and so Gericke took command, as the most senior surviving officer.

As the paratroopers managed to collect themselves, they started to make their presence felt with the 22nd New Zealand Battalion, under the command of Lieutenant Colonel L.W. Andrew, VC. Andrew had been wary of his mission to defend not only the airfield but also quite a wide area around it, including Maleme village and Hill 107 (also known as Kavkazia Hill). In order to do this, he was forced to spread his companies so thinly that they could not support each other, and he had no reserve with which to react to any crisis. By late afternoon the paratroopers under Gericke had forced their way into the RAF camp, capturing a codebook intact that outlined the Allied order of battle, and were attempting to move east along the road. The two companies under Stentzler eventually made contact with A and B Companies defending Hill 107 and started to exert pressure from the southwest. All this, and the impact of the Luftwaffe bombardment, affected the judgement of Lieutenant Colonel Andrew as to whether his battalion could hold its positions, given the dispersed nature of its deployment. He had been wounded during the air attack and with the increasing fighting all around his perimeter, he called to request that Brigade HQ release the 23rd New Zealand Battalion in order to conduct a counterattack at around 17.00hrs. This request was refused by Brigadier Hargest as both the 22nd and 23rd Battalions were already engaged with paratroopers dropping all over the brigade area.

GENZ GLIDER DETACHMENT LANDING SOUTHWEST OF CANEA, MORNING 20 MAY 1941 (pages 44–45)
The objectives of the 3rd Fallschirmjäger Regiment landing in the central sector included Hania and Souda Bay and so to support this landing, the two remaining companies of the Luftlande Sturmregiment's 1st Battalion would land and eliminate what were considered to be two of the most dangerous anti-aircraft batteries in the area, one the Akrotiri Peninsula, the other about a mile south of Hania. The Akrotiri battery would be the target of Hauptmann Gustav Altmann's No.2 Kompanie landing in fifteen gliders, while the battery just south of Hania was tasked to Leutnant Alfred Genz's No.1 Kompanie in nine gliders, who also had a subsidiary objective of a wireless station in the same area. Unfortunately, Altmann's detachment lost cohesion on the way over and landed in scattered packets all over the peninsula, although one section managed to capture its objective, only to find it was a dummy. This they fortified but were eventually captured when they ran out of ammunition. Leutnant Genz had had something of a premonition as to what would happen on Crete as at the very last minute, just as he was entering his glider at Tanagra, a signaller ran over waving a piece of paper. The message almost made Genz's heart stop – it was an updated intelligence estimate raising the number of Allied personnel on the island from 12,000 to 48,000. Genz, a veteran of the campaign in the Low Countries decided it was a little late for second thoughts, so proceeded on his mission. His detachment lost three of their number on the

way to their objective, two releasing early over Hania, the third exploding when ground fire inadvertently hit a box of grenades, but the remaining DFS 230 gliders (1), which carried nine troops and a pilot, managed to make a landing close to the anti-aircraft site (2), which was near Mournies. It was manned by a troop of the 234th Heavy AA Battery equipped with four 3.7in. anti-aircraft guns (3), who despite their surprise and being armed with only light weapons, such as SMLEs and Webley revolvers (4), tried valiantly to engage the attackers (5). The fight was quickly over however, as glider troops had several major advantages over their parachute brethren. These were that they landed fully armed and equipped, including having MG34 machine guns (6), could go into action very quickly without having lost cohesion in a parachute drop (7), did not have to take time in removing the parachute harness and finally they did not have to scrabble around trying to find weapons containers, which left them vulnerable to Allied fire. After Genz and his detachment had put the anti-aircraft battery out of action, they attempted to reach the wireless station but were prevented from doing so by the 1st Ranger Battalion, supported by Bren gun carriers from the 1st Battalion, the Welch Regiment. After digging in and waiting for relief, Genz decided to move the survivors westwards and after bluffing their way through several Allied checkpoints (Genz spoke very good English and the paratroopers had bare heads) managed to link up with the 3rd Fallschirmjäger Regiment. (Howard Gerrard)

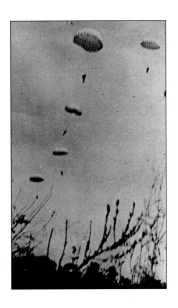

German paratroopers coming down on 20 May 1941, during the battle for Crete. It was in these tense first moments of landing they would be most vulnerable, particularly if the unit was subject to any degree of dispersion, until they found their weapons containers, which were dropped first. (Alexander Turnbull Library, DA-11982)

Andrew then ordered his C Company (Captain S.H. Johnson) to conduct a local counterattack with the support of two tanks, towards the bridge over the Tavronitis. Unfortunately, mechanical failure soon brought their advance to a halt and the counterattack failed. As the day wore on, the situation grew gradually worse for Andrew as he lost contact with his forward companies, was forced to withdraw his headquarters to the reverse slopes of Hill 107, and the wireless communication with Brigade HQ gradually deteriorated. He signalled Hargest that he might have to withdraw his battalion, to which he received the reply 'If you must, you must'. Hargest did, however, signal that two companies were being sent to Andrew's support, and that they would proceed with all haste. Andrew therefore decided to hang on a while longer in the hope that communications with his companies might be re-established, and that some form of relief might arrive.

Elsewhere in the brigade area, the remaining battalions had been kept busy but had gradually gained control of the situation. The New Zealanders had badly mauled Scherber's 3rd Battalion, and so the 23rd New Zealand Infantry Battalion, under Lieutenant Colonel D.F. Leckie, communicated that it was ready to support the 22nd if needed. At around 14.25hrs he received a message from Hargest that so far the reports coming in were satisfactory and they would only be called upon if the situation became serious. While Leckie still had misgivings about Andrew's situation, he held his position and awaited further orders. At around dusk, he did despatch A Company under Captain C.N. Watson to reinforce the 22nd as per Hargest's message to Andrew. The 28th (Maori) Battalion under Lieutenant Colonel G. Dittmer despatched its own B Company under Captain Royal shortly afterwards. The same was true of the 21st New Zealand Infantry Battalion under Lieutenant Colonel J.M. Allen, whose orders allowed some flexibility as to when and where he might launch a local counterattack. His communications were almost non-existent, however, and he could only keep in contact with Leckie by runner. Lack of contact with Brigade HQ left him with very little information on what was happening elsewhere in the brigade area. All he knew was that paratroopers had been seen advancing on Hill 107 from the south, but decided he could not take any action on his own initiative at the moment.

HANIA/PRISON VALLEY – GRUPPE MITTE, FIRST WAVE

The first wave of Gruppe Mitte consisted of the glider detachments under Leutnant A. Genz and Hauptmann G. Altmann. These would land and silence the anti-aircraft guns on the Akrotiri Peninsula, as well as an anti-aircraft battery and wireless station south of Hania. Altmann's detachment became dispersed during the flight and experienced heavier than expected anti-aircraft fire. Finding it difficult to identify their landing sites, they came down widely scattered and were given a rough reception by the companies from the Welch Regiment. The survivors managed to hold out for some time, conducting hit-and-run attacks, but were eventually captured. The smaller detachment under Genz landed and successfully knocked out the AA battery, but could not get near the wireless station. They moved south to join the main body,

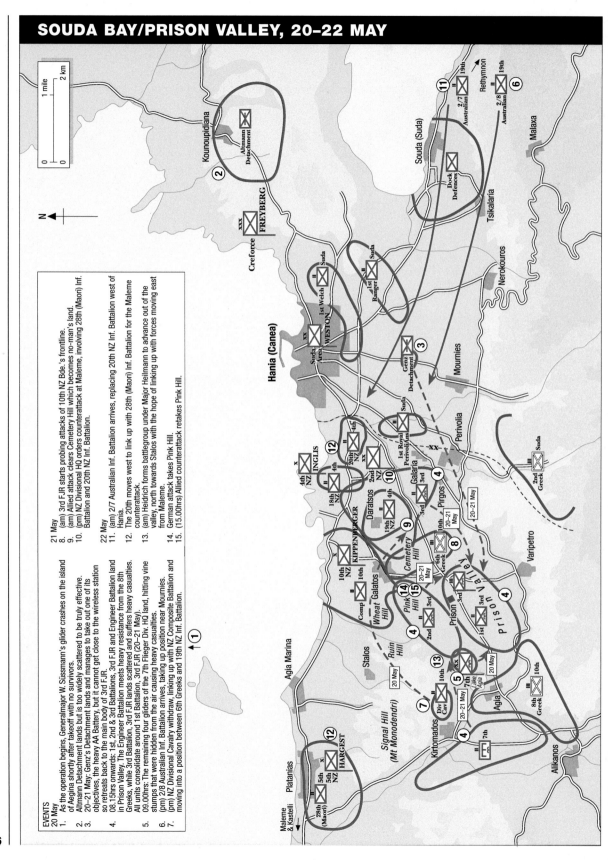

EVENTS

20 May

1. As the operation begins, Generalmajor W. Süssmann's glider crashes on the island of Aegina shortly after takeoff with no survivors.
2. Altmann Detachment lands but is too widely scattered to be truly effective.
3. 20–21 May: Genz's Detachment lands and manages to take out one of its objectives, the heavy AA Battery, but it cannot get close to the wireless station so retreats back to the main body of 3rd FJR.
4. 08.15hrs onwards: 1st, 2nd & 3rd Battalions, 3rd FJR and Engineer Battalion land in Prison Valley. The Engineer Battalion meets heavy resistance from the 8th Greeks, while 3rd Battalion, 3rd FJR lands scattered and suffers heavy casualties. All units consolidate around 1st Battalion, 3rd FJR (20–21 May).
5. 09.00hrs: The remaining four gliders of the 7th Flieger Div. HQ land, hitting vine stumps that were hidden from the air causing heavy casualties.
6. (pm) 2/8 Australian Inf. Battalion arrives, taking up position near Mournies.
7. (pm) NZ Divisional Cavalry withdraw, linking up with NZ Composite Battalion and moving into a position between 6th Greeks and 19th NZ Inf. Battalion.

21 May

8. (am) 3rd FJR starts probing attacks of 10th NZ Bde.'s frontline.
9. (am) Allied attack clears Cemetery Hill which becomes no-man's land.
10. (pm) NZ Divisional HQ orders counterattack at Maleme, involving 28th (Maori) Inf. Battalion and 20th NZ Inf. Battalion.

22 May

11. (am) 2/7 Australian Inf. Battalion arrives, replacing 20th NZ Inf. Battalion west of Hania.
12. (am) The 20th moves west to link up with 28th (Maori) Inf. Battalion for the Maleme counterattack.
13. (am) Heidrich forms battlegroup under Major Heilmann to advance out of the valley, north towards Stalos with the hope of linking up with forces moving east from Maleme.
14. German attack takes Pink Hill.
15. (15.00hrs) Allied counterattack retakes Pink Hill.

46

RETHYMNON, 20–21 MAY

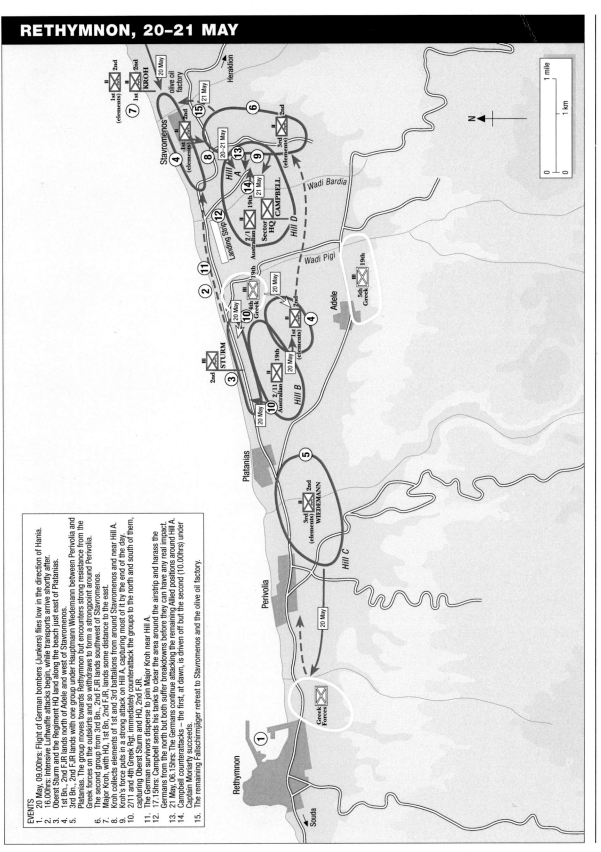

EVENTS
1. 20 May, 09.00hrs: Flight of German bombers (Junkers) flies low in the direction of Hania.
2. 16.00hrs: Intensive Luftwaffe attacks begin, while transports arrive shortly after.
3. Oberst Sturm and the Regiment HQ land along the beach just east of Platanias.
4. 1st Bn, 2nd FJR lands north of Adele and west of Stavromenos.
5. 3rd Bn, 2nd FJR lands with one group under Hauptmann Wiedemann between Perivolia and Platanias. The group moves towards Rethymnon but encounters strong resistance from the Greek forces on the outskirts and so withdraws to form a strongpoint around Perivolia.
6. The second group from 3rd Bn, 2nd FJR lands southwest of Stavromenos.
7. Major Kroh, with HQ, 1st Bn, 2nd FJR, lands some distance to the east.
8. Kroh collects elements of 1st and 3rd battalions from around Stavromenos and near Hill A.
9. Kroh's force puts in a strong attack on Hill A, capturing most of it by the end of the day.
10. 2/11 and 4th Greek Rgt. immediately counterattack the groups to the north and south of them, capturing Oberst Sturm and HQ, 2nd FJR.
11. The German survivors disperse to join Major Kroh near Hill A.
12. 17.15hrs: Campbell sends his tanks to clear the area around the airstrip and harass the Germans from the north but both suffer breakdowns before they can have any real impact.
13. 21 May, 06.15hrs: The Germans continue attacking the remaining Allied positions around Hill A.
14. Campbell counterattacks – the first, at dawn, is driven off but the second (10.00hrs) under Captain Moriarty succeeds.
15. The remaining Fallschirmjäger retreat to Stavromenos and the olive oil factory.

47

making their way through Allied lines thanks to Genz's excellent English.

The gliders were followed at around 08.15hrs by the three battalions of 3rd Fallschirmjäger Regiment under Oberst Richard Heidrich, supported by the Parachute Engineer Battalion and a number of heavy weapons companies. All had good landings but were slightly under strength as problems on the airfields in Greece had reduced the number of transports available. It was quickly realised that the analysis of the available maps and aerial photographs had been inadequate and the Germans found themselves in a shallow valley, rather than on a plateau. Heilmann's 3rd Battalion suffered from a rather dispersed landing and encountered strong resistance from Allied forces in

the area, chiefly elements of the 4th and 10th New Zealand Brigades. Some landed to the north near the 18th New Zealand Battalion (Lieutenant Colonel J.R. Gray), while others dropped around the 6th Greek Regiment and 19th New Zealand Battalion (Major C.A. Blackburn) area. Many of these were captured or killed, but a number landed unmolested to the south and managed to join up with the 1st Battalion. The Engineer Battalion, meanwhile, had a rough reception from the 8th Greek Regiment around Episkopi. However, Heydte's 1st and Derpa's 2nd Battalions landed very well and succeeded in capturing the village of Agia with minimum resistance, where Heidrich set up the regimental command post. They were joined by the survivors of the divisional command post, which had landed nearby in an area dotted with tree stumps that caused severe damage to a number of gliders.

Heidrich quickly consolidated his force and started to probe towards Galatos. After the New Zealand Divisional Cavalry Detachment withdrew from its exposed positions, eventually linking up with the Composite Battalion, Heidrich also established a position on Pink Hill. At this point, Kippenberger was pressing Divisional HQ for reinforcements with which to conduct a counterattack. He expected more paratroopers to be dropped at any moment and to face a serious attack tomorrow. Puttick eventually agreed to a counterattack, after hearing rumours that the Germans were constructing a landing ground, but only by a single battalion and some light tanks from 4th New Zealand Brigade (Inglis). In fact only two companies of the 19th New Zealand Battalion were sent, supported by a troop of light tanks under Lieutenant R. Farran, to cover the possible landing ground with fire, but they had difficulty in finding their way in the darkness and were pulled back after a few brief skirmishes.

By early afternoon, things were looking bleak for the Germans, with the bridge over the Tavronitis being the only objective secured. Casualties were mounting quickly, especially amongst the junior commanders, and many pockets of Fallschirmjäger were pinned down. None of this was known to Generalmajor Student, who ordered the second wave to commence deployment. The German timetable once again began to go wrong as the aircraft had to be refuelled by hand. In addition there was a continuing problem with dust clouds hanging over the runways and

TOP **A photograph showing Ju-52s dropping paratroops into a shallow valley (possibly Prison Valley meaning that the troops are from the 3rd Fallschirmjäger Regiment), and illustrates in stark terms, how low the 'low altitude' drops really were. (B.L. Davis Collection)**

ABOVE **A view from the ground of German paratroopers jumping from Ju-52s onto the island of Crete, 20 May 1941. The airborne assault was of no real surprise to the Allies who had been forewarned by 'Ultra' intercepts of German radio transmissions. This ensured that many of the paratroopers received a rather warm reception. (Alexander Turnbull Library, DA-12638)**

Greek partisan activity, which interfered with the civilian telephone system that the Germans were using to coordinate their flights. The result was that the air support arrived over the island some time before the second wave of Fallschirmjäger. The paratroopers' aircraft were also forced to take off in small groups with the result that the Fallschirmjäger were delivered in penny packets spread over several hours.

RETHYMNON – GRUPPE MITTE, SECOND WAVE

At Rethymnon, the second wave of Gruppe Mitte, some 1,500 strong, consisted of the 2nd Fallschirmjäger Regiment (less the 2nd Battalion) under Oberst Alfred Sturm, supported by a powerful force of ancillary troops. Sturm had divided his force into three groups: the first based around the 1st Battalion under Major Kroh, the second based around the 3rd Battalion under Hauptmann Weidemann reinforced with an Machine gun Company, and the third around the Regiment HQ under Sturm himself. The unit dropped on top of part of the 19th Australian Brigade and the 4th and 5th Greek Regiments. The drop was again scattered but at least they faced fewer opponents than at Heraklion. However, in this case the widely dispersed drop and the incomplete information used for planning worked in the Germans' favour. Two companies of the 3rd Battalion landed to the west of the 19th Brigade's positions, formed up and headed west towards their objective at Rethymnon. They unexpectedly ran into fierce resistance from civilians and the Greek Gendarmerie, and so were unable to take the town. Rather than take heavy casualties in mounting a frontal attack, Weidemann decided to fall back and establish a strong defensive position around the village of Perivolia.

The remaining two companies of the 3rd Battalion and two companies from the 1st Battalion dropped around the 2/1 Australian Battalion's

German paratroopers from the 1st Fallschirmjäger Regiment dropping around Heraklion after the area had been 'prepared' by fighters and bombers from Fliegerkorps VIII, 20 May 1941. A Ju-52 is on fire while it continues to drop troops. A large equipment load, distinguished by three parachutes, is visible on the left of the photograph, such a load would probably consist of either a light artillery piece or vehicle. (Alexander Turnbull Library, DA-02061)

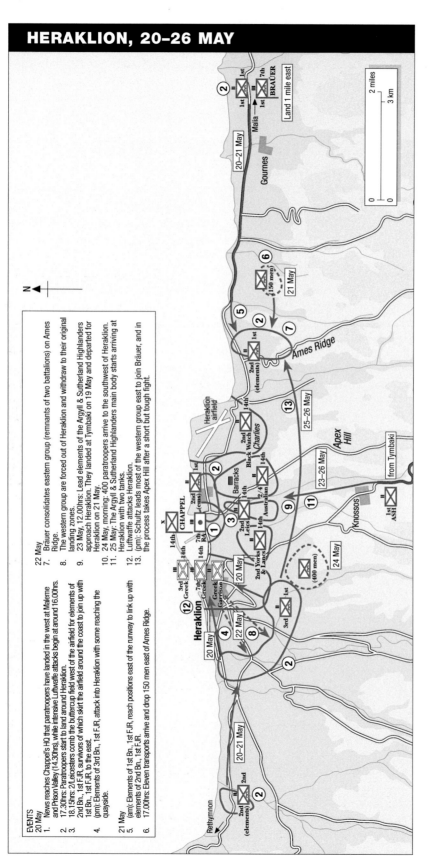

EVENTS

20 May
1. News reaches Chappel's HQ that paratroopers have landed in the west at Maleme and Prison Valley (14.30hrs), while intensive Luftwaffe attacks begin at around 16.00hrs.
2. 17.30hrs: Paratroopers start to land around Heraklion.
3. 18.15hrs: 2/Leicesters comb the buttercup field west of the airfield for elements of 2nd Bn., 1st FJR, survivors of which skirt the airfield around the coast to join up with 1st Bn., 1st FJR, to the east.
4. (pm): Elements of 3rd Bn., 1st FJR, attack into Heraklion with some reaching the quayside.

21 May
5. (am): Elements of 1st Bn., 1st FJR, reach positions east of the runway to link up with elements of 2nd Bn., 1st FJR.
6. 17.00hrs: Eleven transports arrive and drop 150 men east of Ames Ridge.

22 May
7. Bräuer consolidates eastern group (remnants of two battalions) on Ames Ridge.
8. The western group are forced out of Heraklion and withdraw to their original landing zones.
9. 23 May, 12.00hrs: Lead elements of the Argyll & Sutherland Highlanders approach Heraklion. They landed at Tymbaki on 19 May and departed for Heraklion on 21 May.
10. 24 May, morning: 400 paratroopers arrive to the southwest of Heraklion.
11. 25 May: The Argyll & Sutherland Highlanders main body starts arriving at Heraklion with two tanks.
12. Luftwaffe attacks Heraklion.
13. (pm): Schultz leads most of the western group east to join Bräuer, and in the process takes Apex Hill after a short but tough fight.

German paratroopers from the 3rd Fallschirmjäger Regiment being dropped near Galatos, 20 May 1941. The photographer is probably from the 10th New Zealand Brigade, under Colonel Howard Kippenberger, which defended the area around Galatos, Ruin Hill, Wheat Hill and Cemetery Hill. (Alexander Turnbull Library, DA-01178)

Photograph by E. Rowe showing Junkers Ju-52 transport aircraft dropping paratroopers, probably from the 3rd Fallschirmjäger Regiment during the initial stages of the invasion, 20 May 1941. Depending on how quickly they exited the aircraft, the height at which they jumped and the wind conditions, paratroopers such as these could be spread over a wide area. (Alexander Turnbull Library, DA-11017)

positions, while the 3rd Company (1st Battalion) and the Battalion HQ under Kroh landed away to the east. The 2nd Company and the Regimental HQ landed right in the middle of the Allied positions and faced rapid counterattacks from the Australians and the Greeks, directed by Lieutenant Colonel Ian Campbell, who as well as commanding the area retained command of his own battalion the 2/1. Sturm and his HQ were captured. The Germans to the east assembled quickly and moved westwards to support their comrades. This force under Major Kroh managed to put in a strong attack and succeeded in taking the majority of Hill A, which overlooked the eastern end of Rethymnon airfield. They dug in but faced numerous Australian counterattacks. Campbell attempted to use his tanks in one attack but one tank became stuck in a gully, and the other fell into a ravine some eight feet deep. As the day wore on, it became increasingly critical for Campbell to counterattack and dislodge the Germans on Hill A. He contacted Freyberg with a request for reinforcements but was told that none were available – he was on his own. He resolved to counterattack with everything he had at first light the next day.

HERAKLION

The 1st Fallschirmjäger Regiment under Oberst Bruno Bräuer, reinforced with the 2nd Battalion, 2nd Fallschirmjäger Regiment and additional support troops (in all, almost 3,000 men), dropped around Heraklion and suffered as much as any of the other formations dropped that day. The Heraklion area was far easier to defend than the Maleme area, allotted to the New Zealand Division west of Hania, as it was smaller and both the town and the airfield could be enclosed within a perimeter some four miles across and two miles deep. While the defenders at Heraklion did not start to receive word of the parachute drops further west until shortly before Bräuer and his men started landing, a warm welcome would still be waiting for them. Accounts differ as to exactly when word started to reach Brigade HQ but it seems to have started to filter through between 14.30 and 15.00hrs as no alert seems to have been issued from

These two recently landed paratroopers, probably from the 3rd Fallschirmjäger Regiment, look towards the smoke rising above Souda Bay. One carries a Mauser Kar 98k rifle and MP40 sub-machine gun on his back, while the other has hefted his MP40 onto his shoulder. While the Kar 98k had a longer range and greater accuracy, the MP40 was more compact, lighter and had a higher rate of fire, making it more suitable for airborne troops. (B.L. Davis Collection)

Dust and smoke is kicked up during the Allied counterattack towards Maleme airfield, early on 22 May 1941. The counterattack involved both the 20th New Zealand and 28th (Maori) Battalions advancing westward along the coast road and the 21st New Zealand Battalion advancing northwest towards Hill 107. (Alexander Turnbull Library, DA-03466)

Brigade HQ before then, with many British officers still on official and unofficial business away from their units.

The paratroopers of the 1st Fallschirmjäger Regiment dropped onto and around the 14th Infantry Brigade, commanded by Brigadier B.H. Chappel. The 2nd Battalion under Hauptmann Burckhardt dropped from west to east across the airfield following the line of the coast road and were caught in a crossfire between 2nd Leicesters, 2/4 Australian Battalion and 2nd Black Watch. Small arms and anti-aircraft fire greeted the transport aircraft and paratroopers as they fell, mainly into open spaces with little cover. This meant that it was easier to locate the all-important weapons containers, but considerably riskier to try and retrieve them. Under orders from Chappel, the 2nd Leicesters sent out fighting patrols around 18.15hrs, supported by a few Bren carriers to clear the 'Buttercup Field'. However, several groups of paratroopers had managed to assemble and took cover in a number of abandoned buildings. They were left to be taken care of later. The 3rd Battalion under Hauptmann Karl-Lothar Schulz managed to drop just west of the town without too much trouble and started to move eastwards, encountering elements of the Greek Garrison Battalion and groups of civilians at the Hania Gate. These had to be overcome before the Fallschirmjäger could move into the town itself. The 1st Battalion under Major Erich Walther landed with the Regimental HQ further to the east and was relatively intact. Bräuer quickly sensed that the landing had run into trouble, however; to drop single battalions in this way had been a mistake. The Regimental HQ and the 1st Battalion quickly assembled and moved westwards to join up with whatever remained of the 2nd Battalion. The 2nd Battalion, 2nd Fallschirmjäger Regiment, under

Smoke and dust rises above Maleme airfield during the initial assault by the glider detachments and 4th Battalion, LLSR (approaching from the left of the picture), 20 May 1941. The photograph is probably taken from the hills south of the airfield, occupied by the 22nd New Zealand Battalion. (Alexander Turnbull Library, DA-10999)

Photographed by Lance Corporal Goodall, these German paratroopers lay close to their glider, the door of which can be seen in the background. It is unclear as to whether they died in the crash or were killed leaving it but these are the same bodies as shown in an earlier picture and it can be seen that one has his boots removed, possibly by scavenging Allied troops. (Alexander Turnbull Library, DA-12685)

2ND BATTALION, 1ST FALLSCHIRMJÄGER REGIMENT LANDING JUST WEST OF HERAKLION AIRFIELD, AFTERNOON, 20 MAY 1941 (pages 56–57)

Heraklion was to be the target for Gruppe Ost, consisting of Oberst Bruno Bräuer's 1st Fallschirmjäger Regiment, reinforced with a battalion from Oberst Alfred Sturm's 2nd Fallschirmjäger Regiment and strong supporting units. The plan was for the 2nd Battalion, 2nd Fallschirmjäger Regiment (Schirmer) to land well to the west of Heraklion and along with the 3rd Battalion, 1st Fallschirmjäger Regiment (Schulz) who would land to the southwest, would take the town itself. The 2nd Battalion, 1st Fallschirmjäger Regiment (Burckhardt) would drop in two battlegroups to the east and west of the airfield and capture that while the 1st Battalion, 1st Fallschirmjäger Regiment (Walther) would land some five miles east of Heraklion along with the Regimental HQ, capture the radio station at Gournes and act as regimental reserve. All of this was to happen immediately after the support from Fliegerkorps VIII had done its work with all the formations dropping at the same time. Unfortunately due to the chaos on the airfields in Greece, this proved very difficult to organise and the Fallschirmjäger were dropped over a period of several hours. Intense rifle and anti-aircraft fire erupted (1) as the Ju 52s (2) swept round in their flat 'V' formations of three, to drop the Fallschirmjäger. Allied troops on two small hills, nicknamed 'the Charlies', were firing almost horizontally at the transports as they flew past. Much of Burckhardt's battalion dropped along the line of the coast road, over almost every British and Dominion unit in the garrison. Many Ju-52s were

hit (3) but only fifteen aircraft were lost, although it must be remembered that this was double the combined losses at Maleme, Prison Valley and Rethymnon. The eastern battlegroup landed on the edge of the defence perimeter of the Black Watch and managed to set up a position at the foot of Ames Ridge. The western battlegroup however, landed in an area known as 'Buttercup Field' (4) and struggled to attain cohesion and locate their weapons containers (5) to set up any sort of defence. Unlike the terrain around Maleme and in Prison valley, there were few trees or telegraph poles that could potentially snag parachutes, but there was precious little cover of any description. Those that landed in the open spaces had to free themselves from their harnesses (6) and make for the weapons containers in almost full view of the Allied troops, whereas those that landed in more favourable terrain such as the rough ground near the airfield stood a marginally better chance of survival. Unlike his counterparts in the west, Brigadier Chappel immediately counterattacked with every unit at his disposal, including the 2nd Battalion, the Leicestershire Regiment and the 2nd Battalion, the Black Watch (7), who were supported by two Matilda tanks, and eliminated the remaining Fallschirmjäger in the Buttercup Field and around the airfield. He neglected however, to occupy a number of buildings on either side of the coast road and around the airfield (8). These were soon turned into makeshift strongpoints that had to be dealt with later. Of the western battlegroup, only five survivors managed to escape by jumping into the sea and swimming around the coast to join up with the 1st Battalion. (Howard Gerrard)

A large group of German prisoners, some of whom are wounded, being held in a street in Hania. They are probably from the various detachments of the 3rd Fallschirmjäger Regiment that landed near the city on 20 May. They would not have long to wait until the tables were turned. (IWM – E3066E)

Hauptmann Gerhard Schirmer, dropped unscathed even further to the west[2] to act as a blocking force on the coast road. Chappel had lost no time in counterattacking, but remained on the defensive as he was unsure exactly how many paratroopers had landed in the area and whether there might be more on the way. For the time being he would wait to be reinforced by the 1st Battalion, Argyll and Sutherland Highlanders, and organise a counterattack into Heraklion to drive out Schulz's 3rd Battalion who had managed to gain a foothold in the town.

NIGHTFALL, 20 MAY

By the end of the first day, the Fallschirmjäger were hanging on by their fingernails. Had Freyberg used his superiority in men and matériel to counterattack at this point, he might have caused the entire German operation to collapse. Alternatively if he had appreciated the significance of the fighting around Maleme and reinforced the airfield subsequent events may have been very different. Hindsight is a marvellous thing, however, and at the time the situation must have been deeply worrying for Freyberg. He had received a series of reports of huge numbers of enemy Fallschirmjäger dropping all along the north coast of the island and all his garrisons were under attack simultaneously. The picture was made worse by rumours and reports that were difficult to verify due to the increasing problems of both communication and transport that were plaguing the defenders. Two examples of these rumours illustrate the point admirably: the first was that the Germans were constructing a landing strip in Prison Valley, the second that they had landed transport aircraft in the bed of the Tavronitis, as well as on the beaches. The latter rumour probably originated with the glider landings by the detachments under Von Plessen and Braun. Such rumours also served to distract Allied attention from the critical importance of the airfields to the German operation. This was precisely the picture that Student, despite Löhr's

---

2 Part of 2nd Battalion, 2nd Fallschirmjäger Regiment, had to be left behind in Greece due to the lack of space on the available transports.

German mountain troops on their way to Maleme airfield on Crete inside a Ju-52, photographed by Dr K. Bringmann. They were to reinforce the paratroopers after they had captured an airfield. (Alexander Turnbull Library, DA-11979)

desire to concentrate the Fallschirmjäger on a single target, had hoped to contrive.

Nevertheless, Student was in a difficult position. As far as he could ascertain, things had gone badly just about everywhere. Heraklion had not fallen, and there was no news, which almost certainly meant bad news, from Rethymnon. There was not a single location anywhere securely in German hands at which the waiting Gebirgsjäger could be landed. However, many of the Allied anti-aircraft and field artillery guns had been silenced, and those that remained were concentrated in the east. Fliegerkorps VIII was pounding the Allies effectively by day, disrupting any daylight counterattacks. The only possible opening was in the west at Maleme where the Luftlande Sturmregiment had a toehold at both the western end of the runway and the foot of Hill 107.

The withdrawal at Maleme

What the Germans were not to discover until the next day was that Lieutenant Colonel Andrew had decided to withdraw the remains of his battalion from their perilously exposed positions. He had been under continued pressure from Stentzler's companies to the south, lost contact with his forward companies and Brigade HQ, seen no sign of the promised reinforcements and received an at best unhelpful message from Hargest. He sent out runners to contact his companies, but those making for C, D and Headquarters Companies do not seem to have got through. Andrew then withdrew to a ridge east of Hill 107 where he met up with A Company, 23rd Battalion. B Company from the 28th had reached as far as the airfield, to within 200 yards of the 22nd Battalion's C Company command post, but then having heard German voices, decided that their positions had been overrun and withdrew. Andrew then felt that his position was still too exposed and took the decision to withdraw one kilometre east to a position between the 21st and 23rd Battalions. This move was copied in turn by the remaining companies of the 22nd who, after losing contact with Battalion HQ, received reports

An interesting photo of a group of Fallschirmjäger taking cover on some stone steps behind a wall. The man on the left carries a cine camera, while the paratrooper on the right is using a rangefinder. An anti-tank rifle, probably a Panzerbüsche 39, sits just in front of them. It fired a 7.92mm solid tungsten-carbide round and could penetrate 1.3in. of armour at 325ft. The generally relaxed look of the group indicates that this might be a posed shot. (B.L. Davis Collection)

from stragglers that the Battalion HQ had gone. This one decision handed the battle to the Germans (unless a successful counterattack was launched) as direct fire could no longer be brought down on the airfield, and the Germans could start to reinforce the Fallschirmjäger with the 5th Gebirgs Division.

The capture of Hill 107

This process would begin only slowly, however, as there was still sporadic indirect fire coming down on the airfield and, for a while, the Germans did not realise the New Zealanders had vacated their positions. What clinched German control of the airfield was the decision by Dr Heinrich Neumann, the senior medical officer in the Luftlande Sturmregiment, to form a combat group of paratroopers from whoever happened to be close to the regimental aid post and assault Hill 107. A combat veteran of the Spanish Civil War, Neumann had flown over 20 missions as a rear gunner in a Condor Legion Heinkel biplane until told to concentrate on his medical duties! The decimation of the Sturmregiment's officers gave Neumann an unexpected opportunity to once again play an active combat role, and a crucially important one. After telling his assistants to carry on without him, he headed off for Hill 107. He encountered a company of paratroopers under Leutnant Horst Trebes who joined him, and a series of accidental clashes in the dark with Allied troops followed. This episode was subsequently reworked as a story of savage fighting and heroic conquest by an unconventional leader, who later received the Knight's Cross. What was important, however, was that through Neumann's initiative the Germans discovered that Hill 107 was now unoccupied and took control of both it and the airfield.

21 MAY

Meanwhile Student had spent a sleepless night in the Hotel Grande Bretagne studying maps and the reports coming from Maleme. He

noticed that if Hill 107 had been taken, transports could land on the western edge of the airfield out of sight of the defenders. To test his theory, Student dispatched a Ju-52 with a staff officer, Hauptmann Kleye, on board. The aircraft landed at dawn on 21 May and luckily the western edge of the airfield did indeed prove to be dead ground, shielding the plane from the New Zealand defenders. Kleye was briefed on the situation and took off again. At 08.00hrs, six aircraft landed on the runway with ammunition and supplies badly needed by the Fallschirmjäger. These aircraft also lifted out a number of the badly injured, including Eugen Meindl. At this point, Student decided to switch his point of maximum effort from Heraklion to Maleme. With Meindl evacuated, Student gave command of the Sturmregiment to Oberst Bernhard Ramcke, he was dropped with those Fallschirmjäger who had not landed the previous day. The paratroopers landed both west and east of the airfield, to respectively reinforce the Sturmregiment and take the defenders in the rear. Unfortunately, it does not seem to have occurred to Student that those dropping to the east might suffer the same fate as Scherber's 3rd Battalion the previous day. The result was largely the same and the Fallschirmjäger once again suffered serious casualties, although the survivors fortified the village of Pyrgos on the road between the airfield and Hania. Those to the west dropped without incident and Ramcke started to re-form the Sturmregiment as a fighting unit. After this, a steady stream of Ju-52s shuttled in and out of Maleme, with the troops from the 100th Gebirgsjäger Regiment starting to arrive from around 17.00hrs.

Meanwhile, the German positions elsewhere on the island proved to be relatively stable. In Prison Valley, the 3rd Fallschirmjäger Regiment, having been resupplied with almost 300 containers, continued to

ABOVE, LEFT **Photograph by R.T. Miller showing a dead German paratrooper, probably from 10th Company, 3rd Battalion, 3rd Fallschirmjäger Regiment, who had tried to set fire to the hospital marquee at the British General Hospital near Galatos. He was shot dead by New Zealand troops while trying to escape. (Alexander Turnbull Library, DA-01108)**

ABOVE **Members of the 5th Field Ambulance unit attend to wounded German paratroopers, probably from the LLSR, under some olive trees on Crete shortly after the invasion started. The 5th Field Ambulance had been stationed near Agia Marina but had moved to a position near Modi in mid-May. It is possible that the medic is taking down details to be passed on to the Red Cross, as the paratrooper is now a prisoner of war. (Alexander Turnbull Library, DA-09598)**

A group of Fallschirmjäger moving forward in the foothills of Crete. It is possible they are from the 3rd Fallschirmjäger Regiment advancing towards the Allied positions near Perivolia, 26 May 1941. The terrain of Crete quickly became more rugged as one moved inland from the coast. (B.L. Davis Collection)

conduct probing attacks along 10th New Zealand Brigade's front, while a local New Zealand attack, supported by Roy Farran's tanks, managed to dislodge an advanced German outpost from Cemetery Hill, which appropriately enough became a no man's land. One heartening episode occurred after the attacks on Pink Hill, as the paratroopers under Heidrich settled into their defensive positions. One of Heydte's platoons that was encamped on a small ridge across the valley from the 2/8 Australian Battalion, played dance music on a captured gramophone. When one of the desultory exchanges of fire with the Australians lasted longer than usual, one of the paratroopers shouted 'Wait a minute, while I change the record!' At Rethymnon, the German forces under Major Kroh continued in their attempts to eliminate the few remaining Allied positions on Hill A, but were forced to retreat after Lieutenant Colonel Campbell launched the second attack of the day at 10.00hrs, the first at dawn having failed. The survivors retreated to form a position around Stavromenos and the olive oil factory. Despite Allied attacks over the next few days, the groups in both the olive oil factory and Perivolia were dug in and proved difficult to evict from their positions. When an Australian attack, supported by some field guns, did penetrate the factory, all they found were German wounded; Kroh and everyone who could walk had escaped.

Around Heraklion, 150 men, unable to land the previous day, landed east of Ames Ridge at around 17.00hrs and reinforced the remnants of the 1st and 2nd Battalions, 1st Fallschirmjäger Regiment, under Bräuer who had established a position on the ridge. As the days wore on, the killing became less impersonal to the British and Australians, and their enemy became less abstract and more human. A tacit agreement was reached that, during the relative quiet of the night, the wounded could be collected, the dead buried and supplies distributed.

In one episode reminiscent of Steven Spielberg's film *Saving Private Ryan*, three German brothers fighting on Crete were caught up in the tragic consequences of war. One outpost that survived from the first day's drops consisted of a platoon led by Leutnant Count Wolfgang von

Blücher, a name not unknown to the British Army. It held a position in the midst of the Black Watch. According to the account of the story, the Fallschirmjäger, running short of ammunition and medical supplies, were amazed to see a rider and horse galloping towards them with boxes of supplies. The soldiers of the Black Watch were similarly stunned and only opened fire at the last moment, hitting both horse and rider. Von Blücher asked who the rider was, to be told it was his younger brother Leberecht, and that he was dead. The next morning Wolfgang, the eldest of three brothers, was killed as the survivors of his platoon were overrun, despite attempts by the main German forces to the east to come to their aid. The youngest brother, Hans-Joachim, was also killed on Crete but his body was never recovered. For many years afterwards, a number of poor families living in a shanty village in the area reported seeing a ghostly horse and rider, but assumed that the rider was a British officer.

Major Schulz's battalion, after being forced away from the town on 22 May, consolidated their positions and were reinforced by a drop of some 400 remaining paratroopers on the morning of the 25th. Schulz then received orders from Athens to join up with Bräuer by means of an extended march to the south of the Allied positions. This he did late on the evening of 25 May, taking Apex Hill on the way.

What the Germans feared most at this point was a strong local counterattack to force them away from Maleme airfield. Certainly there were enough forces in the area with the 21st, 22nd, 23rd and 28th (Maori) New Zealand Battalions, along with the 4th New Zealand Brigade as yet uncommitted near Hania. Unfortunately for the defenders, the continued air bombardment, the surprise at a novel form of warfare, the absence of good communications and the presence of pockets of the 3rd Battalion, Luftlande Sturmregiment, which were still active and intent on making a nuisance of themselves, all tended to pin the defenders to their positions disrupting the flow of information and orders and rendering swift, decisive action practically impossible.

The Royal Navy intercepts the German convoys

At sea, the continued presence of a large number of Royal Navy ships had, until the 'Ultra' revelations, seemed inexplicable in the face of complete Luftwaffe air superiority, but it is now known that signals intelligence had warned the British that the initial force from the 5th Gebirgs Division (3rd Battalion, 100th Gebirgsjäger Regiment) were on their way to reinforce the Fallschirmjäger. The convoy had left Piraeus harbour on 19 May and had reached the island of Milos the next day where they rested. It left Milos the following day as the second group left Piraeus. At around 23.00hrs it was located by a Royal Navy force of three cruisers and four destroyers just as it rounded Cape Spatha and despite the valiant efforts of an Italian destroyer, sank the majority of the convoy with heavy casualties in an engagement that lasted some two and a half hours. The 3rd Battalion ceased to be an effective fighting force with around 250 survivors being picked up from the water, although a single transport managed to make it to Cape Spatha with 3 officers and 110 men. The following day at around dawn, another Royal Navy force (four cruisers and three destroyers) located the second convoy, but that managed to retreat while the Luftwaffe distracted the British ships who had to withdraw under the increasing pressure of German air attack. The

Luftwaffe then mounted a major offensive against any British ships that could be found and sank two cruisers and four destroyers, as well as damaging three more ships.

Allied counterattack at Maleme, 21–22 May

Starting to recognise the seriousness of the situation at Maleme, Freyberg decided to launch a major night attack to drive the Germans from the airfield. Still worried about a seaborne invasion, however, he failed to quickly commit the two available New Zealand Battalions (18th and 20th). Instead he attempted to move the remaining Australian battalion from around Georgioupolis to relieve the 20th that would then move forward to reinforce the 28th, a somewhat convoluted move given the need for swift action. This was despite 2nd Lieutenant Cox, an officer on his staff and a journalist in civilian life, finding a faded operations order for the 3rd Fallschirmjäger Regiment amongst a bundle of captured German documents. The accuracy with which it detailed the German analysis of how the fighting would unfold left no doubt as to whether the document was genuine or not. Indeed, it outlined very clearly the need to seize the airfields as quickly as possible and that there would be no attempt to land transports in open country.

The plan for the counterattack had first been discussed by field telephone on the morning of 21 May as there were signs that the 3rd Fallschirmjäger Regiment were preparing to advance north to try and cut off both the 5th and 10th Brigades, a factor that had influenced the move of the 2/8 Australian Battalion to a position between the 'Royal Perivolians' and the 2nd Greek Regiment late on 20 May. Freyberg then called a conference at 'Creforce' HQ in the afternoon to ensure that everyone understood that the 2/7 Australian Battalion from Georgioupolis would replace the 20th New Zealand Battalion guarding the coast before the latter moved. The final decision on the operation was taken around 18.00hrs and it seems no one raised the issue that two battalions might be insufficient to oust an enemy that was being reinforced by transports

Two Fallschirmjäger continue marching along a track leading over the lower slopes of the mountain range covering the centre of Crete. Judging by the parachute hanging in the background, this is close to one of the original dropping zones. One is armed with a Panzerbüsche 39 anti-tank rifle, the other with a Mauser Kar 98k. The anti-tank rifles used by the Fallschirmjäger could be effective against lightly armoured vehicles but would be useless against the likes of a Matilda tank. (B.L. Davis Collection)

A group of German Gebirgsjäger advance in column. It is unlikely that they expect to make contact with Allied forces in the near future given their general disposition, and so it is possible that they are on the flank of the German advance, probably from 85th Gebirgsjäger Regiment. Photograph from the book *Gebirgsjäger auf Kreta*. (Alexander Turnbull Library, DA-12651)

landing every few minutes. Brigadier Vasey was somewhat taken aback by the decision to deploy his one remaining battalion westwards, as he had planned to use it to clear the road to Rethymnon and reinforce Campbell's forces there. Lieutenant Colonel T.G. Walker, CO of the 2/7, expressed his concerns over such a move in daylight, but they were dismissed by Brigadier Inglis. Freyberg thus turned the operation over to Brigadier Edward Puttick, who failed to concentrate additional forces to support Hargest. Despite their best efforts, the Australians arrived late due to delays in assembling their vehicles and the attentions of the Luftwaffe, and did not relieve the 20th New Zealand Battalion until after 23.30hrs. As a result, the 20th did not join the Maoris on the start line until almost 03.00hrs, with the result that the operation did not begin until 03.30hrs. The planned attack on Pyrgos and the airfield would not take place until daylight when the Luftwaffe was in a position to intervene.

The 20th New Zealand Battalion advanced westwards to the north of the coast road, Roy Farran's tanks drove along the road while the Maoris advanced to the south of the road and the 21st New Zealand Battalion tried to advance towards Hill 107 from the southeast. The New Zealanders ran into the remnants of the 3rd Battalion that were hiding in the rough ground to the east of the airfield with the survivors of the drops the day before and so the attack started to bog down, with a series of house-clearing actions. The Maoris encountered less opposition to begin with but then encountered some strong defensive positions and also came to a halt amid fighting in and around the German strongpoint in Pyrgos. Farran's tanks managed to advance to the edge of the town, but one was knocked out by a captured Bofors while another halted with mechanical failure. The first company to reach the airfield was D Company of the 20th Battalion, by then under Lieutenant Maxwell, which found the German defenders under Oberst Ramcke ready and waiting for them, and so decided to withdraw despite the gradual arrival of the rest of the battalion. The 21st New Zealand Battalion, on the southern flank, managed to make some headway against the German mountain troops but, after reaching a position near Vlaheronitissa, could not continue unsupported. The counterattack had failed, with the New Zealanders exhausting themselves in the process.

THE GERMAN ADVANCE FROM MALEME

By this time on the afternoon of 22 May, the Germans were rapidly reinforcing their troops on Crete with the 5th Gebirgs Division, despite the continued artillery fire targeted on the airfield. Transports were landing at a rate of 20 per hour and two fresh Gebirgsjäger battalions arrived that afternoon. The 5th New Zealand Brigade therefore pulled back from its forward positions at Pyrgos, barely a mile from Maleme, covered by a company of Maoris under Major H.G. Dyer. Generalmajor Julius Ringel arrived, and from this point on the Gebirgsjäger assumed responsibility for a greater proportion of the fighting. Ringel divided the German forces at Maleme into three Kampfgruppe (battlegroups) – the 95th Gebirgs Pioneer Battalion under Major Schätte was to defend Maleme and gradually push westwards to capture Kastelli. The reconstituted Luftlande Sturmregiment, now known as Kampfgruppe Ramcke, was to advance to the sea and then push eastwards along the coast, while two battalions (1st and 2nd) of the 100th Gebirgsjäger Regiment and a battalion (1st) from the 85th Gebirgsjäger Regiment, under the command of Oberst Willibald Utz, were to trek eastwards over the mountains in the hope of outflanking the Allied positions.

This plan was put into operation the next day, 23 May. The paratroopers under Ramcke advanced slowly eastwards out of the village of Pyrgos, discovering the remnants of Scherber's 3rd Battalion, and the reinforcements dropped on 21 May. Forward elements managed to reach Platanias Bridge by 11.00hrs and set up defensive positions. They were subjected to a counterattack from elements of D Company, 28th (Maori) Battalion, under Captain F. Baker, but successfully held their line. The Gebirgsjäger under Oberst Utz moved into the mountains but by the afternoon had been stopped at the village of Modi, where the New Zealanders had established a blocking position. Fierce fighting erupted around the Modi position and the New Zealanders were forced to pull back as elements of the Gebirgsjäger outflanked them. This meant that the covering artillery had to withdraw to a more secure position and so Maleme airfield was finally free of Allied artillery fire. Heidrich sent a fighting patrol out northwards in the early hours under Major Heilmann to make contact with the advancing mountain troops. The detachment took the village of Stalos at dawn and despite a counterattack by a company from the Composite Battalion and B Company, 18th Battalion, managed to retain possession of the village.

The German advance was also hindered by elements of the 8th Greek Regiment and by Cretan irregulars. They successfully held up both the main advance by the mountain troops and the motorcycle-mounted 95th Reconnaissance Battalion. The latter was heading for

Some Fallschirmjäger, after leaping over a stone wall in their path, then move quickly towards the nearest available cover. It is unlikely that troops in action would leap over a stone wall into an unknown area so it is possible that this is a posed shot. (B.L. Davis Collection)

GERMAN ADVANCE ON PLATANIAS

23 May 1941, viewed from the northeast showing the advance on Platanias by the reconstituted Luftlande Sturmregiment (now Ramcke Group), 100th and 85th Gebirgsjäger Regiments and 3rd Fallschirmjäger Regiment, threatening to outflank 5th New Zealand Brigade.

Note: Gridlines are shown at intervals of ½ mile/0.8km

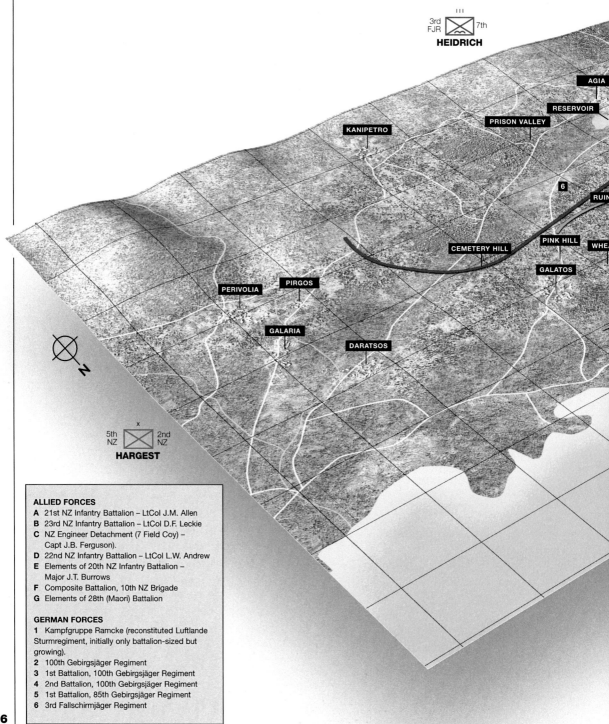

ALLIED FORCES

A 21st NZ Infantry Battalion – LtCol J.M. Allen
B 23rd NZ Infantry Battalion – LtCol D.F. Leckie
C NZ Engineer Detachment (7 Field Coy) –
Capt J.B. Ferguson).
D 22nd NZ Infantry Battalion – LtCol L.W. Andrew
E Elements of 20th NZ Infantry Battalion –
Major J.T. Burrows
F Composite Battalion, 10th NZ Brigade
G Elements of 28th (Maori) Battalion

GERMAN FORCES

1 Kampfgruppe Ramcke (reconstituted Luftlande Sturmregiment, initially only battalion-sized but growing).
2 100th Gebirgsjäger Regiment
3 1st Battalion, 100th Gebirgsjäger Regiment
4 2nd Battalion, 100th Gebirgsjäger Regiment
5 1st Battalion, 85th Gebirgsjäger Regiment
6 3rd Fallschirmjäger Regiment

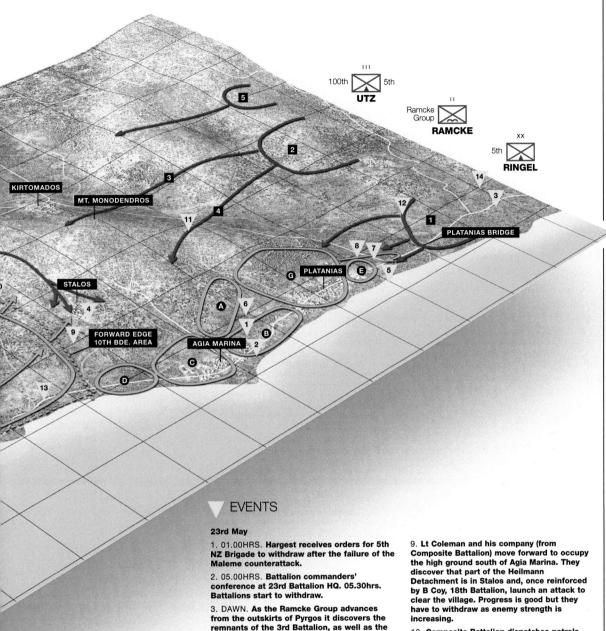

KIRTOMADOS

MT. MONODENDROS

STALOS

FORWARD EDGE
10TH BDE. AREA

AGIA MARINA

PLATANIAS

PLATANIAS BRIDGE

100th ⊠ 5th
UTZ

Ramcke
Group ⊠
RAMCKE

5th ⊠⊠
RINGEL

▼ EVENTS

23rd May

1. 01.00HRS. **Hargest receives orders for 5th NZ Brigade to withdraw after the failure of the Maleme counterattack.**

2. 05.00HRS. **Battalion commanders' conference at 23rd Battalion HQ. 05.30hrs. Battalions start to withdraw.**

3. DAWN. **As the Ramcke Group advances from the outskirts of Pyrgos it discovers the remnants of the 3rd Battalion, as well as the reinforcements dropped on 21 May.**

4. **The Heilmann Detachment of 3rd Fallschirmjäger Regiment seizes Stalos.**

5. AROUND 08.45HRS. **Elements of 28th (Maori) Battalion cross Platanias Bridge, watched by Lt Farran and Squadron SgtMaj Childs.**

6. 10.00HRS. **The battalions settle into their new positions.**

7. 11.00HRS. **28th (Maori) Battalion rearguard crosses the river just south of the Platanias Bridge under fire by forward elements of the Ramcke Group.**

8. **A group under Capt F. Baker (second in command, D Coy, 28th (Maori) Battalion) that had been ordered forward to hold the bridge area, attacks and gets close to the bridge putting a gun out of action but has to withdraw due to enemy fire.**

9. **Lt Coleman and his company (from Composite Battalion) move forward to occupy the high ground south of Agia Marina. They discover that part of the Heilmann Detachment is in Stalos and, once reinforced by B Coy, 18th Battalion, launch an attack to clear the village. Progress is good but they have to withdraw as enemy strength is increasing.**

10. **Composite Battalion dispatches patrols under Capt Nolan and Lt Carson.**

11. 12.00HRS. **2nd Battalion, 100th Gebirgsjäger Regiment reaches the Platanias River.**

12. 14.55HRS. **Germans are seen fortifying positions around Platanias Bridge and soon after begin shelling 28th (Maori) Battalion positions. The Germans start to concentrate for an assault, while continuing probing attacks.**

13. 15.15HRS. **Brig Puttick orders 5th NZ Brigade to withdraw as it is in danger of being cut off by German flanking movements.**

14. 15.55HRS. **RAF aircraft attack Maleme.**

15. 22.00HRS. **5th NZ Brigade starts to withdraw into divisional reserve.**

67

A German light anti-aircraft gun (2cm Flak 30) stands guard over the airfield at Maleme while Ju-52s continue to land troops and supplies. After capturing the airfield on 21 May, the Germans rapidly built up their forces and reinforced the anti-aircraft defences against expected Allied air strikes, which occured several times after the airfield fell. (Alexander Turnbull Library, DA-11983)

A German Unteroffizier (Sergeant) from the 100th Gebirgsjäger Regiment pauses by a stone wall in the renewed advance into Galatos, 26 May 1941. Nearby are Allied casualties lying in a ditch running beside the road, as well as Lieutenant Roy Farran's destroyed light tank further up on the left. (Alexander Turnbull Library, DA-12652)

Paleochora on the south coast to prevent the Allies landing reinforcements there. The Greeks and Cretan irregulars were so successful that they may well have played a decisive part in preventing a substantial part of the New Zealand Division from being surrounded. In its advance towards Kastelli, the 95th Gebirgs Pioneer Battalion under Schätte came up against fierce but uncoordinated resistance from both the 1st Greek Regiment and armed civilians including women and children.

For many Germans there was an added horror in fighting the Cretans, as they believed that the locals had no qualms about mutilating German dead or wounded that fell into their hands. Although the Germans eventually announced they would execute ten Cretans for every mutilated German they found, it had little apparent effect. Student's intelligence officer, Major Johannes Bock, led a military commission that concluded that many of the apparent mutilations were a result either of the particular type of combat encountered on Crete or of the post mortem attentions of birds or animals.

The Pioneer Battalion, along with the survivors of Mürbe's detachment that had been captured after they had dropped outside Kastelli, finally captured the town on 25 May. Continued Cretan resistance meant it was not until 27 May that it could be used to land tanks.

By 24 May, the Germans were being reinforced on a huge scale and their supply state was such that they could begin to adopt conventional tactics, supported by tactical air power and their own artillery. The fact that the Germans had transported artillery onto the island came as a great surprise to the Allies. This was unheard of in 1941, with artillery considered far too cumbersome and heavy for airborne operations, but the Germans overcame this obstacle by deploying one of Europe's first recoilless guns.

The first very basic recoilless gun had been invented by an American naval officer, Commander Davis, during the First World War. Davis reasoned that if two guns were placed back to back and fired simultaneously, the recoil from both would cancel each other out. He made a gun with a single central chamber and two barrels facing in opposite directions. One barrel carried an explosive projectile, the other an equivalent weight of grease and lead shot. When the central cartridge was exploded the two projectiles were sent down their barrels at identical speeds making the entire mechanism free from recoil. The explosive shell went to its target while the wad of grease and shot disintegrated in the air. The Davis gun was purchased by the British, who undertook experiments to see if it could be used as an anti-submarine weapon, but the war ended before the trials were completed. A German company, Rheinmetall, continued to experiment with the idea and eventually reduced it to a much simpler form. Reasoning that recoil could still be counterbalanced if the ejected 'countershot' were smaller but faster, they found that the shell could be counterbalanced by a stream of gas moving at very high speed through a nozzle in the gun breech. The LG40 was a 75mm calibre gun, weighing 320lbs, which fired a 13lbs high explosive shell to a range of 6.8km. The German Army's conventional 75mm gun weighed 2,470lbs and fired the same shell to a range of 9.4km. Thus the recoilless rifle allowed virtually the same firepower as a conventional artillery piece, with two thirds the range but one eighth of the weight.

Galatos falls

By the end of 24 May, the German formations heading east from Maleme had finally united with Heidrich's men to form a cohesive front to the west of the Allied lines. These had moved again late on 23 May. Puttick was aware of the threat to the Allied right flank from the advancing German mountain troops. As a result, 5th New Zealand Brigade had again withdrawn eastwards; this time into divisional reserve and the 10th New Zealand Brigade took over responsibility for the frontline. Kampfgruppe Ramcke, 100th Gebirgsjäger Regiment and the 3rd Fallschirmjäger Regiment faced them in a line running inland roughly southeast from the coast. Now the Germans had reached the New Zealand blocking position at Galatos, they started a series of aggressive probing attacks, particularly against the Composite Battalion

GERMAN ADVANCE ON GALATOS

24–26 May 1941, viewed from the northeast. Heavily reinforced, German forces sweep east from Maleme towards Galatos and Hania. Allied attempts both to stem the German tide and to form a new defence line ultimately prove unsuccessful.

Note: Gridlines are shown at intervals of ½ mile/0.8km

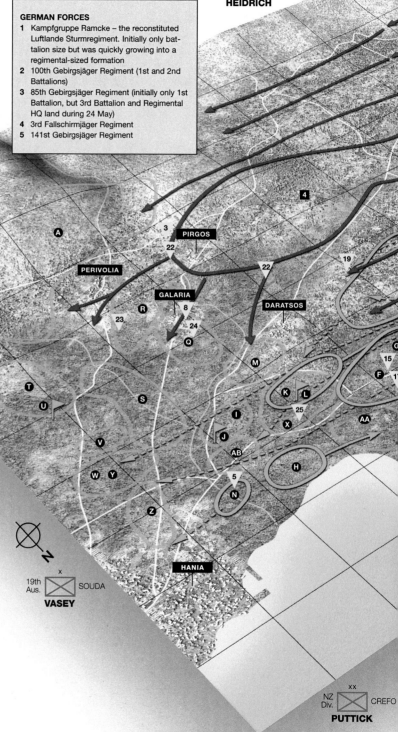

ALLIED FORCES

- **A** 2nd Greek Regiment
- **B** 6th Greek Regiment
- **C** 8th Greek Regiment
- **D** 18th NZ Infantry Battalion (24 May) – LtCol J.R. Gray
- **E** 19th NZ Infantry Battalion – Maj C.A. Blackburn
- **F** 20th NZ Infantry Battalion – Maj J.T. Burrows
- **G** 4th NZ Brigade HQ – Brig L.M. Inglis
- **H** 21st NZ Infantry Battalion – LtCol J.M. Allen
- **I** 22nd NZ Infantry Battalion – LtCol L.W. Andrew
- **J** NZ Divisional HQ – Brig Puttick
- **K** 23rd NZ Infantry Battalion – LtCol D.F. Leckie
- **L** 5th NZ Brigade HQ – Brig J. Hargest
- **M** 28th (Maori) Infantry Battalion – LtCol G. Dittmer
- **N** NZ Engineer Detachment – Capt J.B. Ferguson
- **O** Composite Battalion – MajH.M. Lewis
- **P** Russell Force (Divisional Cavalry and Petrol Coy) – MajJ.T. Russell
- **Q** 2/7 Australian Infantry Battalion – LtCol T.G. Walker
- **R** 2/8 Australian Infantry Battalion – Maj A.S. Key
- **S** Royal Perivolians
- **T** Royal Marine Battalion
- **U** 19th Australian Brigade HQ – Brig G.A. Vasey
- **V** 1st Echelon Divisional Supply
- **W** 18th NZ Infantry Battalion (26 May)
- **X** 19th NZ Infantry Battalion (26 May)
- **Y** Composite Battalion (26 May)
- **Z** 20th Battalion (26 May)
- **AA** 21st Battalion Group (26 May)
- **AB** 23rd NZ Battalion (26 May)

GERMAN FORCES

- **1** Kampfgruppe Ramcke – the reconstituted Luftlande Sturmregiment. Initially only battalion size but was quickly growing into a regimental-sized formation
- **2** 100th Gebirgsjäger Regiment (1st and 2nd Battalions)
- **3** 85th Gebirgsjäger Regiment (initially only 1st Battalion, but 3rd Battalion and Regimental HQ land during 24 May)
- **4** 3rd Fallschirmjäger Regiment
- **5** 141st Gebirgsjäger Regiment

▼ EVENTS

1. 24 MAY. 85th Gebirgsjäger Regiment continues to cautiously advance against 8th Greek Regiment. (1)

2. 24 MAY. The Luftwaffe attacks Galatos. (2)

3. 05.30HRS, 24 MAY. 2nd Greek Regiment conducts a local attack against the Turkish Fort just east of Pirgos. (3)

4. MORNING, 24 MAY. 100th Gebirgsjäger Regiment links up with Heilmann's detachment near Stalos. (4)

5. MORNING, 24 MAY. NZ Engineer Group is broken up, with 19th Army Troops Company going to 19th Australian Brigade, while 7th Field Company goes to 20th NZ Infantry Battalion. (5)

6. 14.00HRS, 24 MAY. A strong enemy probe is beaten off with artillery fire near Wheat Hill. (6)

7. 16.00HRS, 24 MAY. 1st Battalion, 100th Gebirgsjäger Regiment conducts a reconnaissance in force towards Red Hill supported by artillery and machine-gun fire from Ruin Hill. (7) This is repeated at dusk.

3rd FJR / 7th — HEIDRICH

PIRGOS
PERIVOLIA
GALARIA
DARATSOS
HANIA

19th Aus. / SOUDA — VASEY

NZ Div. / CREFO — PUTTICK

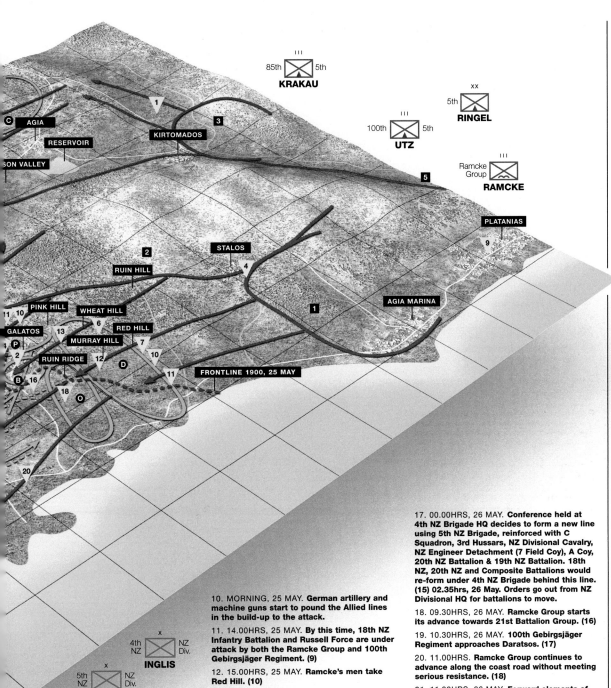

85th [X] 5th
KRAKAU

xx
5th [X]
RINGEL

100th [X] 5th
UTZ

Ramcke
Group [X]
RAMCKE

C AGIA
RESERVOIR
SON VALLEY
KIRTOMADOS
1
3
5
PLATANIAS
9
STALOS
2
RUIN HILL
4
AGIA MARINA
1
PINK HILL
11 10
WHEAT HILL
6
RED HILL
GALATOS
13
7
MURRAY HILL
2
P
RUIN RIDGE
12
10
D
B 16
11
FRONTLINE 1900, 25 MAY
18
O
20

4th
NZ [X] NZ
Div.
INGLIS

5th
NZ [X] NZ
Div.
HARGEST

8. AFTERNOON, 24 MAY. 2/7 and 2/8 Australian Battalions conduct aggressive patrolling and some minor skirmishes occur. **(8)**

9. 19.15HRS, 24 MAY. Ringel issues orders for an attack, with 85th Gebirgsjäger Regiment taking the area around Alikanos and then heading east, while 100th Gebirgsjäger Regiment and Ramcke Group capture Galatos and the area north of it. As the attack develops, 3rd Fallschirmjäger Regiment will move east, maintaining contact with 100th Gebirgsjäger Regiment to its left and 85th Gebirgsjäger Regiment to its right.

10. MORNING, 25 MAY. German artillery and machine guns start to pound the Allied lines in the build-up to the attack. **(9)**

11. 14.00HRS, 25 MAY. By this time, 18th NZ Infantry Battalion and Russell Force are under attack by both the Ramcke Group and 100th Gebirgsjäger Regiment. **(9)**

12. 15.00HRS, 25 MAY. Ramcke's men take Red Hill. **(10)**

13. 16.00–17.00HRS, 25 MAY. D Coy, 18th Battalion is overrun, while A, B and C Coys are forced to retreat. Ramcke Group occupies Murray Hill, while 2nd Battalion, 100th Gebirgsjäger Regiment occupies Wheat Hill. **(11)**

14. 18.10HRS, 25 MAY. 1st Battalion, 100th Gebirgsjäger Regiment fully joins assault. Russell Force withdraws. German troops enter Galatos at around dusk. **(12)**

15. 19.30HRS, 25 MAY. 20th, 21st & 23rd NZ Infantry Battalions are ordered forward. **(13)**

16. AROUND 20.00HRS, 25 MAY. C & D Coys, 20th Battalion and elements of 18th & Composite Battalions counterattack into Galatos supported by tanks. **(14)**

17. 00.00HRS, 26 MAY. Conference held at 4th NZ Brigade HQ decides to form a new line using 5th NZ Brigade, reinforced with C Squadron, 3rd Hussars, NZ Divisional Cavalry, NZ Engineer Detachment (7 Field Coy), A Coy, 20th NZ Battalion & 19th NZ Battalion. 18th NZ, 20th NZ and Composite Battalions would re-form under 4th NZ Brigade behind this line. **(15)** 02.35hrs, 26 May. Orders go out from NZ Divisional HQ for battalions to move.

18. 09.30HRS, 26 MAY. Ramcke Group starts its advance towards 21st Battalion Group. **(16)**

19. 10.30HRS, 26 MAY. 100th Gebirgsjäger Regiment approaches Daratsos. **(17)**

20. 11.00HRS. Ramcke Group continues to advance along the coast road without meeting serious resistance. **(18)**

21. 11.30HRS, 26 MAY. Forward elements of 21st Battalion Group withdraw under air and mortar attack. They are engaged by Ramcke Group soon after. **(19)**

22. 12.00HRS, 26 MAY. 3rd Fallschirmjäger Regiment begins attack in the southern sector. **(20)**

23. 17.00HRS, 26 MAY. 2/8 Australian Battalion is forced to withdraw, moving in the direction of Mournies. **(21)**

24. 18.30HRS, 26 MAY. 2/7 Australian Battalion is fully engaged. **(22)**

25. 22.30HRS, 26 MAY. Puttick orders 19th Australian Brigade & 5th NZ Brigade to withdraw due to German pressure, the withdrawal starting at 23.30hrs.

This group of paratroopers appears to be pushing a 37mm anti-tank gun along a Cretan road, while the paratrooper at the rear carries a box of ammunition. The gun was designed by Rheinmetall in 1935 and adopted by the Wehrmacht, being designated the PAK 35/36. It could penetrate 48mm of armour plate at 457m but a new tungsten-cored ammunition (AP40), introduced in 1940, increased penetration to 51mm. (B.L. Davis Collection)

and Russell Force (the amalgamated New Zealand Divisional Cavalry and Petrol Company under Major J. Russell).

This led to a general attack on 25 May, with pressure quickly building in the late afternoon from the south and west. It was the 18th New Zealand Battalion that had to give way first; the right-hand company was overrun by Ramcke's men at around 18.00hrs, despite a gallant counterattack led by Lieutenant Colonel Gray. After some bitter fighting, the Composite Battalion disintegrated as well, with troops streaming down the road towards Hania. A German breakthrough was only narrowly averted by inserting part of the 20th Battalion, which had moved forward on orders from Inglis. The collapse spread down the line from Wheat Hill, however, and soon the entire 18th Battalion was withdrawing, although Russell Force remained in its positions, partially cut off. After the New Zealanders had been ejected from Galatos by the Germans, Kippenberger attempted to rally as many troops as he could for a counterattack, including two companies from the 23rd New Zealand Battalion, the 4th New Zealand Brigade band, some Pioneers and the Kiwi Concert Party. These were joined by Captain Michael Forrester and Lieutenant Roy Farran with two light tanks. Following an initial reconnaissance by the two light tanks, this most composite of composite forces charged into Galatos, and after some bitter fighting, successfully evicted the Germans, enabling the survivors of Russell Force to withdraw. Their mission accomplished, the New Zealanders withdrew during the night under orders from Kippenberger, allowing the Gebirgsjäger to occupy the village and open the way for an advance on Hania. That night, a very tired Kippenberger made his way to the 4th New Zealand Brigade command post, where the remaining battalion commanders had already arrived. Inglis raised the question of counterattacking again, and Lieutenant Colonel Dittmer volunteered his 28th (Maori) Battalion. After a general discussion, it was decided that the time had passed, and that the only course would be to withdraw to a position adjoining Brigadier Vasey's 19th Australian Brigade. Even though nobody dared speak of it openly, it looked as though their ultimate fate would once again be in the hands of the Royal Navy.

A group of retreating Allied troops pushes a truck over the bank during the withdrawal to Sphakion on the south coast. This is taken from an 8mm film, shot by John Gray. A large number of vehicles were abandoned on the retreat to Sphakion either due to running out of fuel, being damaged by enemy air attack or simply not be able to move any further after reaching the end of the road. (Alexander Turnbull Library, DA-12183)

The new line just west of Hania held on 26 May, aided by the Luftwaffe's accidentally bombing a battalion of the 85th Gebirgsjäger Regiment. This shook German morale and induced an understandable caution in their advance. The battalion in question had been pressing east in the foothills near Perivolia towards the area held by the 2nd Greek Regiment, which was beginning to dissolve. North of the Greeks was the 19th Australian Brigade, once again consisting of the 2/7 and 2/8 Infantry Battalions. From here north to the coast were three New Zealand battalions, reduced in strength and semi-amalgamated. Holding the German advance here would allow the Royal Navy to offload essential stores that night, as well as allowing the main body of Layforce (two battalions of commandos) to land, commanded by Colonel Robert Laycock. This force had discovered that, despite assurances in Alexandria that the battle was going well, the reality was very different.

The destruction of Force Reserve

Meanwhile, despite Force Reserve (the Welch Regiment, Northumberland Hussars and the Rangers) being placed under Inglis' command, General Weston gave orders that Force Reserve was to advance westwards and replace the exhausted 5th New Zealand Brigade just west of Hania. He failed, however, to give the New Zealanders orders to withdraw when replaced. Nor does he seem to have been aware that the Australians had by then been outflanked and were under pressure to withdraw. No one seemed to know which units were under the command of which headquarters. Puttick and Hargest were becoming frustrated by a lack of orders and Freyberg was away from his command post, visiting the dockside at Souda. Puttick countermanded Freyberg's order that the Australians should stand fast come what may, ordering both Hargest and Vasey to retreat to a new line along what was now known as '42nd Street' while they still had the cover of darkness. He did not realise that Force Reserve was already moving westwards and would now be advancing unsupported against a superior enemy force.

Maleme

Ramcke Group
RAMCKE
100th — 5th
UTZ
3rd — 7th
HEIDRICH
141th — 5th
JAIS
85th — 5th
KRAKAU

27 May

Hania (Canea)

Sternes

Force Reserve
1

27 May: Breakout

Perivolia
Mournies
Nerokouros
Malaxa
2
27 May

1st — 141st
19th Australian
5th NZ

Souda (Suda)

Advanced guard WITTMANN
Megala Khorafia (Megali Horafia)
Kalami
3
A — Layforce
Kalives
28th (Maori) (elements)
1st — 85th
28 May
2nd — 85th
5th NZ
4
Stilos
2/7 Australian
28 May
28 May
2/8 Australian
Armeni
Kalives

WAG
3rd — 85th
2nd — 85th
D — Layforce Kaina
Babali Hani
2/8 Australian
2/7 Australian
5
28 May
Permonia
Fres
Nippos
Vamos
6
141st — 5th

Vrysses
7
18th NZ — 28 May
Wittmann Advanced guard
85th — 5th KRAKAU
8
141st JAIS
Embrossneros
2nd — 100th Alikambos
1st — 100th
Rethymnon & Heraklion

23rd NZ
29 May
9
18th NZ
2/8 Australian
29 May
29 May
Sin Ammoudari
Sin Kares
Sin Petres
10
4th NZ
29 May
2nd — 100th
1st — 100th
Imbros
11

30 May
2/8 Australian
21st NZ
Kommitades
2/7 Australian
Royal Marines
30 May
Layforce

Sfakion (Sphakion)

N

| 0 | 3 miles |
| 0 | 5 km |

EVENTS

27 May

1. The Germans deploy five regimental-sized combat teams (north to south – Ramcke Group, 100th Gebirgsjäger Regiment, 3rd Fallschirmjäger Regiment, 141st Gebirgsjäger Regiment, and 85th Gebirgsjäger Regiment) that push east. Ramcke Group, 100th Gebirgsjäger Regiment and 3rd Fallschirmjäger Regiment encircle Force Reserve, some elements of which breakout and rejoin the main force near Souda (Suda). 141st and 85th Gebirgsjäger Regiments continue east.
2. Elements of the 5th NZ and 19th Australian Brigades counterattack the lead elements of 1st Battalion, 141st Gebirgsjäger Regiment in the area of 42nd Street forcing it to retreat. Both Allied brigades start to withdraw around 22.00hrs.

28 May

3. Ringel forms a pursuit force under Oberstleutnant Wittmann. With the help of 1st Bn., 85th GJR, it encircles the Allied rearguard around Megala Khorafia, but some Allied elements manage to withdraw around 12.20hrs. Wittmann's advance guard (WAG) and 1st Bn., 85th GJR, reunite in the afternoon and move south and southeast respectively.
4. 2nd Bn., 85th GJR, makes contact with 5th NZ Brigade and 2/7 Australian Infantry Battalion (Inf. Bn.). The Allied troops withdraw around 10.00–11.00hrs. 2/8 Australian Inf. Bn. to the east withdraws at 11.00hrs.
5. After the failure of an initial attack by 2nd Bn., 85th GJR, and elements of Wittmann's advance guard (WAG), Wittmann's entire force, along with 3rd Bn., 85th GJR, is committed to a second attack. This attack is too late as the Allied rearguard has withdrawn. The Allied rearguard consists of D Battalion, Layforce, and 2/8 Australian Inf. Bn. (arrives 14.00hrs). Both withdraw after 21.00hrs. 2/7 Australian Inf. Bn. arrives around 12.00hrs and continues to withdraw after 13.00hrs, followed by 5th NZ Brigade HQ at 14.30hrs.
6. 141st GJR reaches Vamos in the early afternoon.

29 May

7. 18th NZ Inf. Bn., acting as flank guard, withdraws early morning, 29 May.
8. 100th GJR takes up the pursuit as it arrives, with 1st Bn. in the lead. The German main body (WAG, 141st GJR and 85th GJR) moves east to relieve the Fallschirmjäger at Rethymnon and Heraklion. Ramcke Group and 3rd FJR are left to deal with Akrotiri Peninsula and garrison the Maleme–Hania–Souda area.
9. 1st Bn., 100th GJR makes contact with main Allied rearguard position around 16.30hrs. This consists of 23rd NZ Inf. Bn. (withdraws at 16.30hrs); 18th NZ Inf. Bn. (withdraws at 21.00hrs) and 2/8 Aus Inf. Bn. (remains in contact until 12.00hrs).
10. Defensive positions of 4th NZ Brigade until around 19.00hrs. C Troop, 2/3 RAA engages the enemy from 18.00hrs until dusk.

30–31 May

11. 1st Bn., 100th GJR fans out to positions in the central area, while 2nd Bn., 100th GJR moves up to outflank the Allied positions. The Allied rearguard consists of: 2/8 Australian Inf. Bn., 21st NZ Inf. Bn., 2/7 Australian Inf. Bn., Royal Marines, and Layforce.

The Germans continued their advance, and on 27 May Freyberg took the decision to inform Wavell that, in his opinion, defeat was now inevitable and arrangements should be made to evacuate the Allied forces from Crete. The garrison made preparations to withdraw. During the early hours of the morning, Force Reserve, which had passed through an eerily quiet and deserted Hania, fanned out to the west sending patrols to establish contact with the Royal Perivolians to the south. They discovered that both the Perivolians and the Australians had pulled out. Soon after dawn, Force Reserve heard sounds of fighting well to their rear on the road to Souda. The implication was clear enough.

At this point, the Germans had formed five regimental battlegroups in a line facing the Allies. These were, from north to south, Kampfgruppe Ramcke nearest the coast, 100th Gebirgsjäger Regiment, 3rd Fallschirmjäger Regiment, 141st Gebirgsjäger Regiment and 85th Gebirgsjäger Regiment. The German attack started at 08.30hrs with mortars, artillery fire and machine guns. It soon became clear that Force Reserve had been cut off, with Ramcke's men and the 100th Gebirgsjäger Regiment attacking from the west, while the 3rd Fallschirmjäger Regiment encircled them from the south and the 141st and 85th Gebirgsjäger Regiments continued to advance east towards Souda. Around 250 officers and men managed to fight their way out and make it back to the Allied main force in small groups, but the majority were encircled, to be killed or taken prisoner, the last resistance ending on the morning of 28 May. This was a tragic waste of almost 1,000 fresh troops. The squabbling after the battle, over who was to blame, is reminiscent of the arguments after the Charge of the Light Brigade. Puttick blamed Weston; Weston thought Puttick's countermanding of Freyberg's orders cavalier in the extreme, and Freyberg thought that Inglis had evaded his responsibility to command Force Reserve. Whatever the reason, unclear and badly thought-out orders, poor communications and complicated alterations to the chain of command had invited disaster.

Ringel failed to realise that the Allied forces had withdrawn and thought they were still in position just to the west of Hania, a picture reinforced by the arrival of Force Reserve. The 141st Gebirgsjäger Regiment therefore continued its advance in a southerly arc with the 85th on its right flank, in the hope of encircling a substantial number of Allied troops by cutting the Hania–Souda road. However, the 1st Battalion, at the forefront of the advance, came up against the Australian and New Zealand positions at the 42nd Street line at around 11.00hrs. A spontaneous counterattack started, taking the Germans by surprise, and 1st Battalion, 141st Gebirgsjäger Regiment, was badly mauled but managed to retreat to a position supported by the 3rd Battalion. Both the 141st and 85th Gebirgsjäger Regiments paused, surprised at this reverse. By standing firm, the 5th New Zealand and 19th Australian Brigades had managed to buy time for the retreat to get under way.

THE ALLIED RETREAT TO SPHAKION

That afternoon, nearly 30 hours after he had originally outlined that defeat was now inevitable, Freyberg received confirmation from Wavell to go ahead with his plan to withdraw south over the mountains to Sphakion. Wavell initially wanted Freyberg to withdraw east to link up with the garrisons at Rethymnon and Heraklion. Freyberg suspected that was what Ringel was expecting him to do, however, and Wavell was forced to agree. That evening, 'Creforce' HQ set off by car and truck over the mountain road to Sphakion.

After Freyberg's departure to Sphakion, Weston was left in command, but his unreliable leadership, not helped by false rumours and bad communications, prompted Vasey and Hargest to formulate their own plans. They withdrew their respective brigades and made a dash for Stilos, to the southeast of Souda on the route to Sphakion. They made it only just in time, as at daybreak on 28 May the 85th Gebirgsjäger

A wounded Allied soldier, possibly from the 28th (Maori) Battalion, disembarks at Alexandria from a destroyer after the Crete campaign, 1 June 1941. (Alexander Turnbull Library, DA-01618)

A line of Allied prisoners of war trudges past advancing German mountain troops from the 100th Gebirgsjäger Regiment, with a selection of vehicles including a fuel bowser, truck, civilian car and motorcycle and sidecar combination. The Allied troops are probably those who did not manage to be evacuated from Sphakion by 31 May 1941. Photograph taken from the book *Gebirgsjäger auf Kreta*. (Alexander Turnbull Library, DA-12646)

Regiment, having renewed its advance some hours earlier and crossed the mountains to cut the Hania–Rethymnon road, ran into the hasty blocking position manned by the 5th New Zealand Brigade, as well as the 2/7 Australian Battalion. The battle raged back and forth but a small Gebirgsjäger force managed to outflank the New Zealand position. The tactics of the Gebirgsjäger consisted of advancing to contact, and once the enemy position had been identified, machine gun and mortar units were sent off to climb prominent features on either flank. This sort of movement took time, but followed Ringel's maxim of 'sweat saves blood'. Artillery and mortars were brought forward to support the renewed attack, which eventually forced the New Zealanders to disengage and retreat south.

Also on 28 May, another battlegroup, Kampfgruppe Wittmann, also known as the Wittmann Advanced Guard (consisting of the 95th Motorcycle Battalion, 95th Reconnaissance Unit, part of the 95th Anti-tank Battalion and some motorised artillery and engineer units) was spearheading the main German advance east. This force was sent along the coast road towards Heraklion to relieve the pockets of Fallschirmjäger that had held out all this time, a number having been reinforced by the drops on 21 and 24 May. Once it reached Heraklion itself it would combine with the Fallschirmjäger and capture the airfield. Kampfgruppe Wittmann managed to advance some three miles beyond Souda but was stopped near Megala Khorafia by a party from A battalion of Layforce (consisting of Spanish Republicans) and some Maoris from the 28th Battalion. The Allied troops were soon forced to retreat to Babali Hani, where the remainder of A Battalion was trying to form another stop line.

AUSTRALIAN COUNTERATTACK AGAINST 1ST BN., 141ST GEBIRGSJÄGER REGIMENT, MORNING 27 MAY 1941

(pages 80–81)

After the Germans had taken Galatos, they could form a solid line of five regimental battlegroups. From north to south these were the Ramcke Group, 100th Gebirgsjäger Regiment, 3rd Fallschirmjäger Regiment, 141st Gebirgsjäger Regiment and the 85th Gebirgsjäger Regiment. They faced a new Allied defence line just to the west of Hania that consisted of the 2nd Greek Regiment in the south, with the 19th Australian Brigade to the north and the three New Zealand battalions of the 5th New Zealand Brigade above them. Force Reserve had been placed under Inglis' command, but despite that, Weston ordered them to move westwards to relieve the exhausted 5th New Zealand Brigade. Unfortunately, he failed to give the New Zealanders instructions to withdraw when relieved and seemed to have learnt that the Australians had been outflanked and were under pressure to withdraw. Puttick and Hargest had become frustrated with the lack of orders and so Puttick decided to countermand Freyberg's order that the Australians should hold come what may, ordering Hargest and Vasey to retreat to a new line based on a sunken track (1) at the Hania (2) end of Souda Bay, known as '42nd Street'. He did not realise that Force Reserve was now in the process of moving westwards and with the eastward movement of the 5th New Zealand Brigade and 19th Australian Brigade, would be advancing unsupported against a superior enemy force. The Germans continued their advance on 27 May with Ramcke Group and 100th Gebirgsjäger Regiment moving directly east towards Hania, 3rd Fallschirmjäger Regiment aiming to swing south of Hania and the 141st and 85th Gebirgsjäger Regiments continuing to move eastwards. All this conspired to place Force Reserve in an enveloping movement, which saw the majority of soldiers captured or killed, although some 250 managed to make it back to the 42nd Street Line. Ringel failed to realise that the main Allied force had in fact withdrawn, a picture reinforced by the appearance of Force Reserve and so continued with the sweeping flanking movement that saw the 141st and 85th Gebirgsjäger Regiment continue eastwards, with a gentle northerly slant. This led the 1st Battalion, 141st Gebirgsjäger Regiment to unexpectedly run right into the 42nd Street Line at about mid-morning. The encounter was simultaneous all along the line and was as much a surprise for the Allies as it was for the Germans. As the Germans advanced, supported by machine guns (3) and mortars, a fierce fire-fight broke out with the leading elements of the Gebirgsjäger battalion falling back. Elements of both 5th New Zealand Brigade and 19th Australian Brigade (4) spontaneously launched a bayonet charge (5) that initiated a round of hand-to-hand combat (6). The Allied troops advanced into the 1st Battalion who held on until two forces had inter-penetrated to some 300 yards and then turned and fled (7), leaving their dead and wounded alongside the Allied casualties (8). By that point, the 3rd Battalion, 141st Gebirgsjäger Regiment had moved up and proceeded to cover the withdrawal of the 1st Battalion. (Howard Gerrard)

The other battalion (D Battalion), which had stayed behind near Souda to delay the enemy, had suffered heavy casualties after two confused engagements, and was in a state of disarray.

The 1st Battalion, 85th Gebirgsjäger Regiment continued to move parallel with Kampfgruppe Wittmann, while the 2nd Battalion made contact with the Allied blocking position around Stilos. However, the two commando battalions had to be amalgamated after the commander of D Battalion virtually suffered a nervous breakdown. Together with the 2/8 Australian Battalion, which had retreated from Armeni with the approach of the 1st Battalion, 85th Gebirgsjäger Regiment, and two Matilda tanks that had arrived from Heraklion, they managed to hold up Kampfgruppe Wittmann and the 2nd and 3rd Battalions of the 85th Gebirgsjäger Regiment around Babali Hani. The Germans eventually forced them to withdraw by flanking the position to the west, after the tanks ran out of fuel.

The evacuation of Heraklion

Soon after dawn on the 28th, the battalion commanders around Heraklion were summoned to Brigadier Chappel's headquarters. There they learned that the battle to the west had turned for the worst and that a Royal Navy squadron would evacuate them from the harbour that night. Secrecy had to be preserved at all costs and although battalion order groups were held at midday, the men were not told until the last moment. For Lieutenant Colonel Pitcairn of the Black Watch, the news that morning was particularly bitter, as one of his most popular company

A destroyer loaded with Allied soldiers arrives in Alexandria from Crete, late May 1941. Naval losses during the campaign had been high, including three cruisers and six destroyers sunk, as well as four capital ships, six cruisers and seven destroyers damaged. It showed the growing importance of airpower for naval operations, a lesson that would also be learned in the Pacific. (Alexander Turnbull Library, DA-09661)

Allied prisoners of war, a photograph taken from the book *Gebirgsjager auf Kreta*. These men are probably from a variety of units, and were eventually transported to prisoner of war camps in both Italy and Germany. Given that the supply situation was somewhat chaotic immediately after the invasion, it is no wonder that many POWs suffered deprivations as they waited to be evacuated. (Alexander Turnbull Library, DA-03405)

commanders, Major Alistair Hamilton, who had promised that 'the Black Watch leaves Crete when the snow leaves Mount Ida', had been killed by a mortar bomb. The feeling in the 14th Infantry Brigade was that the 'other end' had let the side down and that they would be letting down the Cretans who had fought with such bravery. When the men were told at 20.00hrs that evening, many were stunned into silence. To them, the battle had been going well up to that point. There was little time to prepare for the withdrawal, and so a great deal of equipment was destroyed or made unusable including cars, trucks, field guns and signals equipment, while ammunition and petrol stores were booby trapped or buried. A lot of small arms and ammunition were handed over to the Cretans, however, so they could continue their resistance.

The withdrawal was handled perfectly, thanks to the experience of the NCOs in the regular battalions. Oberst Bräuer's paratroopers had no idea what was happening and at 21.30hrs the Allied troops began to withdraw towards the harbour. At 23.30hrs the ships of Admiral Rawling's force reached Heraklion, but contained only two cruisers, HMS *Ajax* having turned back to Alexandria after suffering damage during an air attack. *Orion* and *Dido* remained offshore while the destroyers ferried the Allied troops over to them in pairs. When the cruisers had embarked over 1,000 men each, the destroyers then returned for their passengers. All 3,486 men who had assembled were embarked, by the deadline of 02.45hrs. About an hour and a half after the squadron had set sail, HMS *Imperial's* steering jammed and HMS *Hotspur* was sent back to pick up her crew and passengers, after which she sank *Imperial* with torpedoes. Unfortunately, this led to a delay as the force waited for *Hotspur* to catch up and was thus still short of the Kaso Strait and the island of Skarpanto with its enemy airfield. When the sun finally rose at around 06.00hrs, the first wave of attackers was spotted against the dawn sky. The attacks continued for some six hours. *Hereward* was hit first and tried to beach on Crete. The *Orion* was attacked twice and received two direct hits and several near misses. Two bombs penetrated three decks and caused devastation where the 1,000 soldiers were sheltering. Some 260 men were killed and a similar number wounded. The NCOs who had volunteered to man Bren guns to help with the anti-aircraft defence had made a fortunate choice. *Dido* was also hit twice, with one bomb destroying a gun turret, while the other penetrated the deck, exploding near a canteen packed with soldiers. Over 100 men were killed, either by the blast, by the resultant fire or by drowning when water had to be pumped in to stop the fire spreading to the magazine.

Some men were left behind, such as those in standing patrols or the wounded in Knossos Military Hospital, and those that could joined up with the rear party of Argylls on the south coast. Heraklion was finally occupied on 29 May after German patrols found little resistance.

The fall of Rethymnon

At Rethymnon, Lieutenant Colonel Campbell and his garrison had little knowledge of what was happening on the rest of the island, although a landing craft that had been sent from Souda arrived during the early morning of 28 May. Lieutenant Haig, who commanded it, had not brought Freyberg's instructions for evacuation with him, due to the confusion at Souda and 'Creforce' HQ on the night Layforce had landed. All Haig could tell Campbell was that he was to head for Sphakion on the south coast. Campbell, a regular officer conscious of his responsibility, did not want to abandon his mission to hold the airfield at Rethymnon until he was officially relieved of it. Unfortunately, the two tanks supporting the garrison had been destroyed in an attack on the German strongpoints around Perivolia. Campbell had had to admit there was little chance of clearing the coast road to move westwards and an attack towards Souda was abandoned. Campbell therefore continued with his mission to deny the enemy the use of the airfield as ordered.

Ringel had in fact ordered the bulk of his force to advance to Rethymnon in order to relieve the beleaguered paratroopers there and then to continue to Heraklion. This force was led by Kampfgruppe Wittmann, to be joined eventually by tanks of the 31st Panzer Regiment that had finally landed at Kastelli. After the action around Spilia, they had continued eastward, supported by the 141st and 85th Gebirgsjäger Regiments, entering Rethymnon on 29 May. No further advance was considered possible until armoured cars and artillery were brought up, as the Australians still held positions in the mountains to the south.

That night, Australian soldiers took turns to flash the morse code letter 'A' out to sea in case Royal Navy ships were coming to pick them up. The next day saw the arrival of the German heavy artillery and the start of the bombardment of the Allied positions on the heights surrounding Rethymnon. The German advance from Rethymnon towards the airfield also continued. Campbell, still holding the airfield with his 2/1 Australian Battalion, conferred by field telephone with Major R.L. Sandover, commanding the 2/11 Australian Battalion. Campbell saw little point in continuing hostilities that would lead to futile casualties, especially as food and ammunition were in short supply and so had decided to surrender. Sandover agreed with the futility of continuing to resist but wanted to give every man who wanted to, a chance to escape over the hills. The two officers agreed to differ and went their separate ways. Campbell went into captivity with 700 troops. Sandover, with 13 other officers and 39 NCOs and men, finally managed to escape to Egypt by submarine after spending several months in the mountains.

Members of the 19th New Zealand Battalion on board a destroyer during their evacuation from Crete, 1 June 1941. The 19th had started out with 565 personnel, but by the time of their evacuation were down to some 213. The 19th were to go on and serve in the rest of the North African campaign as part of the New Zealand Division, including taking part in Operation *Crusader*. (Alexander Turnbull Library, DA-10655)

Kampfgruppe Wittmann moved off once again and made contact with a group of Fallschirmjäger from the 2nd Fallschirmjäger Regiment at 09.00hrs, and then at midday with a patrol from the 1st Fallschirmjäger Regiment who had been dug in near Heraklion. The battlegroup then took possession of the airfield where it was joined by a small Italian force that had been landed at Sitia the previous day. It then advanced to the village of Lerapetra on the south coast at 22.00hrs. They encountered few Allied troops, because the main evacuation was in fact taking place further west along the south coast at Sphakion. Allied forces were actually withdrawing to the south and not the east as the Germans had originally assumed. Once they had discovered that the Allied forces were nowhere in sight in the eastern half of the island, the Germans immediately began moving south on 29 May. Those German troops to the east moved south on 30 May.

THE EVACUATION FROM SPHAKION

On the night of the evacuation from Heraklion, the Royal Navy took off the first 1,000 Allied troops from Sphakion in four destroyers. Meanwhile, the Allied main force continued on its trek south, covered in turn by 19th Australian Brigade and the 5th New Zealand Brigade. The troops, weary and thirsty, trudged up the mountain road from Vrysses encountering one ridge after another, but were finally greeted by the sight of the Askifou Plain, a fertile, flat-bottomed valley of fields, meadows and small orchards. By this point, the German advance was led by the two battalions of the 100th Gebirgsjäger Regiment. It was halted by a determined rearguard action by the two Australian battalions under Vasey, the 23rd New Zealand Battalion and the last three light tanks of the Hussars. The action at Babali Hani had made the Germans wary of taking risks, but with the end now in sight the mountain troops had adopted a somewhat light-hearted approach. Many had discarded their winter jackets and trousers, wearing odd items of British tropical clothing, which occasionally caused confusion. A somewhat bizarre situation occurred when the Germans took the village of Askifou and raided the richest house in the village, owned by a newly married couple. The Gebirgsjäger proceeded to wear the new wife's embroidered knickers and petticoats on their heads, to act as improvised protection from the baking sun. They looked more like a chorus line in a regimental concert troop than frontline soldiers.

At the southern end of the Askifou Plain lay the Imbros Pass, which offered a reasonably safe descent to the coast. The road continued for a few more kilometres and then came to a sudden stop on a massive bluff overlooking the sea. The last precipitous stretch of road lay along what was little more than a goat track winding down the rock face. Abandoned vehicles lay all around, a testament to the failure of the military authorities to finish the road.

'Creforce' HQ had been established in a cave in the rock face below the road. Puttick arrived at the cave at last light on 29 May, having been summoned by Freyberg who told him to leave the island, as Weston's command of the rearguard made a divisional staff redundant. He saluted Freyberg and said 'We did our best. We did all we could.' The night of 29 May saw the largest evacuation, with Admiral King arriving in HMS *Phoebe*, with the cruisers *Perth*, *Calcutta* and *Coventry*, three destroyers and the commando troopship HMS *Glengyle*, whose landing craft proved to be a godsend. Over 6,000 men were evacuated.

The German advance continued on 30 May as the rearguard withdrew but was checked again at the Imbros Pass. The Germans kept up the pressure however and by the evening of 30 May were less than three miles from Sphakion with the remainder of the island totally in German hands. The 5th New Zealand Brigade descended the escarpment that morning

A photograph by A.J. Spence showing Allied prisoners of war, some of them wounded, waiting to start the journey to Germany and into captivity. They are being held temporarily at the former Allied transit camp at Kokinia, near Piraeus just southwest of Athens, Greece. (Alexander Turnbull Library, DA-12317)

and Hargest, who had shown more determination and sound judgement during the retreat than during the battle, was appalled at the state of the troops that were still there. Half-starved and thirsty base personnel several thousand strong were still encamped in the rows of caves near the beach. As priority in the evacuation went to formed bodies of frontline troops, many tried to beg and implore their way onto the ships, but the New Zealanders had set up a cordon armed with bayonets and sub-machine guns to enforce order. Two destroyers had been forced to turn back that night, so only 1,500 men were taken off. At dawn on 31 May, Admiral King left Alexandria once again with the cruisers *Phoebe* and *Abdiel*, along with two destroyers. After meeting with Wavell, Cunningham decided to risk another sortie to Crete, even though the Mediterranean fleet had been badly mauled by operations around the island. 'It takes the Navy three years to build a new ship' he had declared. 'It will take three hundred years to build a new tradition. The evacuation will continue.' A favourite toast in the wardrooms of the Mediterranean fleet for a long time to come was 'To the three Services, the Royal Navy, the Royal Advertising Federation and the Evacuees.' In their last effort Admiral King's force left Sphakion at 03.00hrs on the morning of 1 June with nearly 4,000 men. They arrived safely, but the anti-aircraft cruiser HMS *Calcutta* was sunk within 100 miles of Alexandria. Major General Freyberg left Crete on 30 May by flying boat. The remaining Allied troops were ordered to surrender at 09.00hrs on 1 June, the surrender being delivered by Lieutenant Colonel Theo Walker to an Austrian officer in the 100th Gebirgsjäger Regiment at Kommitades, leaving the Germans in control of the island.

AFTERMATH

The battle for Crete was a German victory but a costly one. Out of an assault force of just over 22,000 men, the Germans suffered almost 6,500 casualties, of which 3,352 were killed or missing in action. Almost a third of the Ju-52s used in the operation were damaged or destroyed. The British and Commonwealth forces suffered almost 3,500 casualties (of which just over 1,700 were killed) and almost 12,000 were taken prisoner (including Lieutenant Colonel Walker's 2/7 Australian Battalion), while the Greeks had approximately 10,000 men taken prisoner. The Royal Navy lost three cruisers and six destroyers sunk, and one aircraft carrier, two battleships, six cruisers and seven destroyers were badly damaged, with the loss of over 2,000 men. The RAF lost some 47 aircraft in the battle. Exactly how many Greek soldiers and Cretan civilians died during the fighting will never be known.

There were positive lessons to be learned from the battle, such as the importance of air power in providing support to the ground troops and its impact on naval operations. Superior German leadership and initiative also contributed to the outcome. However, it is the failings by both sides that deserve most attention. The use of intelligence and the performance of command and control structures were the key to the evolution of the battle for both the Germans and Allies.

The German airborne forces were relatively well equipped but their operational planning was flawed due to poor intelligence. The lack of surprise resulted in high casualties and brought the operation perilously close to failure. Had it not been for the support of Von Richthofen's Fliegerkorps VIII and the leadership and initiative qualities shown by the German officers, particularly the junior commanders, the battle would have been lost.

The numerically superior but poorly equipped Allied garrison lost the battle by only a slim margin, due to the fact that the key commanders involved failed to understand both the threat from and the vulnerabilities of an airborne force. They also missed the opportunity to launch an aggressive counterattack. Throughout the battle, the Luftwaffe utilised its immense advantage in combat power to help restrict the impact made by the Royal Navy, support the beleaguered paratroopers, demoralise the defenders and interdict Allied troop movements. The casualty figures show a higher than usual killed-to-wounded ratio, a testament to the ferocity of the battle and how close the result was.

As a result of the huge losses suffered by the Fallschirmjäger in Crete, it was forbidden to mount any large-scale operations in the future, with Hitler telling Student on 19 July 1941 that the day of the paratrooper was over. Apart from a few small-scale operations, the paratroopers mainly served as elite infantry for the rest of the war. Crete was rightly dubbed the 'Graveyard of the Fallschirmjäger' with Student in 1952 admitting that 'For me, the Battle of Crete … carries bitter memories.'

The Gebirgsjäger who were drafted into the operation at the last moment performed admirably, as they did throughout the war. The fact that the operation was undertaken just three weeks after the fall of Greece is a testament to the flexibility, ingenuity and determination of the German armed forces who had to overcome immense logistical difficulties.

British operations on Crete were hampered by the poor shape many units found themselves in after the campaign in Greece. Indecision, misunderstanding, a lack of information (at least when the fighting started) and poor communications in the chain of command, both on Crete itself and from Crete to Egypt, also played a part. The order to Freyberg to preserve the airfields for the future use of the RAF also proved misguided. The importance and reliability of the 'Ultra' intercepts was not apparent to Freyberg as the exact source of the information was not revealed to him. As such he continued to focus primarily on the threat of an amphibious attack. There was no clear-cut plan of defence, and what was undertaken was done so at the last minute. The defence of the island was improvised and with the British at full stretch in the rest of North Africa and the Middle East, the men and matériel necessary for the defence of Crete could not be spared.

None of the senior commanders performed with distinction. The exception was Cunningham who appreciated the impact of air power on naval operations, the strategic consequences for the Allies of a British defeat at Crete, and the possibility of a shift in the naval balance of power in the Mediterranean. Generally, Allied commanders showed too little aggression and their appreciation of the situation always lagged behind events – something that did not hinder the Germans in the same way, as their commanders led from the front. There was also considerable political interference with Wavell's command from London, specifically from the Prime Minister, Winston Churchill.

In the wake of the final Allied evacuation of Crete on 1 June, and the subsequent surrender of the remaining Allied forces, the occupied island was divided into two zones. The main German zone covered the western provinces of Hania, Rethymnon and Heraklion, while the subsidiary Italian zone covered the provinces of Sitia and Lasithi in the east. The Italian occupation force consisted of the Siena Division, whose commander, Generale Angelo Carta, had his headquarters in Neapolis and ran his zone with a somewhat more liberal and relaxed attitude than many of his German counterparts. The German Garrison HQ was in Hania and its first commandant, General Waldemar Andrae, took over from Student and was in turn succeeded in 1942 by another paratrooper, Bruno Bräuer, former commander of the 1st Fallschirmjäger Regiment. In the spring of 1944, the hated Friedrich-Wilhelm Müller took control, and was to prove the most

Allied troops from the 4th New Zealand Brigade disembark in Alexandria, Egypt after being evacuated from Crete by the destroyer HMS *Nizam*, 31 May 1941. It is obvious that as many men as possible had been put on the ship, which was dangerous under the circumstances as all Allied ships were subject to air attack on their return journey to Egypt. (Alexander Turnbull Library, DA-00399)

brutal of the garrison commanders, a reputation firmly established while in command of the 22nd Luftlande Division at Arhanes, south of Heraklion. The elite 22nd Luftlande Division had been sent to Crete in the summer of 1942 much to the annoyance of a number of senior German officers, who considered it a waste to use such a highly trained division in a garrison role. The garrison strength fluctuated wildly, depending on how the North African and Russian campaigns were progressing and the perception of the threat of invasion. It reached its zenith in 1943 with 75,000 and gradually declined to its lowest of 10,000 just before its surrender on 12 May 1945.

Undoubtedly, the hostile reaction of the Cretan population came as a shock to the Germans as they had expected a more welcoming attitude, the fiercely independent Cretans always having viewed the established Greek government with suspicion and distaste. To the Cretans, however, the Germans were just another invader whom they would fight to defend their homes, island and freedom. Beginning in the summer of 1941, they started to form centres of resistance. The initial aim was to gather as many of the British and Commonwealth troops remaining on the island as possible. The Cretan guerrillas took it upon themselves to protect, feed and clothe these Allied servicemen and, where possible, arrange their safe evacuation so they could carry on the fight elsewhere. For this they needed links with the main headquarters in Cairo and other parts of the Middle East. Over time an effective communications network was established to facilitate not only the evacuation of Allied servicemen, but also the introduction of members of the Special Operations Executive (SOE), to help organise and train the guerrillas, and deliveries of equipment and supplies. For the next four years the Cretan resistance harried the occupying German forces, tying down large numbers of enemy troops that could have been employed elsewhere. The Cretans suffered harsh reprisals as a result, including mass executions and the burning of villages.

This resistance and the help provided by the SOE meant that Crete became the stage for the exploits of a number of extraordinary British servicemen such as Patrick Leigh-Fermor, Dennis Ciclitira, Billy Moss and

Xan Fielding. Perhaps the most famous episode was that immortalised on screen in the film *Ill Met By Moonlight*, starring Dirk Bogarde as Leigh-Fermor. The incident was the capture of General Heinrich Kreipe, commander of the 22nd Luftlande Division by Major Patrick Leigh-Fermor and Captain Stanley Moss with two Greek SOE agents on 26 April 1944. Their original target had been Friedrich-Wilhelm Müller, but as a result of delays in the group's rendezvousing on Crete, Kreipe had replaced Müller. It was decided that the attempt should continue as planned nevertheless. The site for the ambush was a T-junction where the Arhanes road met the Houdesti–Heraklion road, with high banks and ditches on each side. The British officers were disguised as German traffic policemen and could speak German very well. Waving red lamps and traffic signs they flagged the car down and told the driver that the road was unsafe further on. The general was quickly captured and taken prisoner, and when he began to shout was told that he was a prisoner of British commandos and had better shut up. Some of the party then got into the car and drove on with the general until they reached the point where they had to cross the mountains on foot. The commandos left a note in the car that read:

TO THE GERMAN AUTHORITIES IN CRETE
Gentlemen, Your Divisional Commander, General KREIPE, was captured a short time ago by a BRITISH raiding force under our command. By the time you read this, he will be on his way to Cairo. We would like to point out most emphatically that this operation was carried out without the help of CRETANS or CRETAN partisans and that the only guides used were serving soldiers of HIS HELLENIC MAJESTY's FORCES in the Middle East, who came with us. Your General is an honourable prisoner of war and will be treated with all the consideration owing to his rank. Any reprisals against the local population will be wholly unwarranted and unjust.
Auf baldiges Wiedersehen!
P.S. We are very sorry to have to leave this beautiful car behind.

The Germans initially thought that he had been taken by guerrillas and, in a quickly printed leaflet, threatened to raze every village in the Heraklion area to the ground and take severe reprisals against the local population. Patrols and reconnaissance aircraft combed the hills leading south (the most obvious escape route) and in fact occupied the beach that had been selected for the evacuation. Fortunately the commandos heard about this and remained hidden while a new evacuation point was selected. It took the party 17 days to reach the new beach, during which the general fell and his arm had to be put in a sling. The group reached the rendezvous successfully and were taken off safely, reaching Mersa Matruh on the North African coast after a stormy crossing.

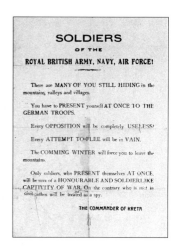

A poster displayed in Crete after the German occupation to try and encourage Allied servicemen to surrender. Many Allied servicemen had gone into hiding rather than surrendering and were cared for by the local population, despite threats of severe punishment. A large number managed to make their way back to Egypt, for example, over 300 were evacuated by submarine alone. (Alexander Turnbull Library, DA-10726)

THE BATTLEFIELD TODAY

The island of Crete is a popular destination for tourists, offering not only golden beaches and blue seas but a long and fascinating history and numerous myths associated with the island. Alongside the reminders of the more recent conflicts of the Second World War are ancient ruins and exquisite works of art, giving a glimpse of Europe's first great civilisation, the Minoans, who built the palace at Knossos, reputedly the home of the mythical King Minos and the Minotaur. There are also the ruins of a Dorian city state, the mighty walls of Venetian fortresses and the towering minarets of Ottoman mosques.

In September 1945, representatives of the New Zealand Division returned to the island to pay their respects and commemorate the battle. On 29 September 1945, 100 officers and men from the New Zealand Expeditionary Force under their commander, Major General Bernard Freyberg attended a memorial service on Crete and spent three days on the island, having been given a fantastic welcome by the local population. By then, the site of the Allied war cemetery had already been chosen (June 1945) and it lies in the north-west corner of Souda Bay, around three miles east of Hania and sheltered to the north by the Akrotíri Peninsula. The cemetery is enclosed with trees and shrubs, has a neatly tended lawn and slopes gently down to the water. It is carefully looked after by three gardeners. The vast majority of those buried here (1,509) were killed in the fighting on Crete, with 19 First World War and 37 other graves having been transferred from the Souda Bay consular cemetery in 1963. Many of the latter graves are not identified as a result of the occupying forces having moved many of the remains from their graves in the fighting areas to four large burial grounds, which they called British military cemeteries. In doing so, the identities of many of the remains were lost. The four burial grounds were at Hania, Heraklion, Rethymnon and Galatos. Commonwealth troops, whose graves are not identified, are commemorated at the Phaleron war cemetery in Athens.

The Souda Bay war cemetery was designed by Louis de Soissons (1890–1962), who designed Welwyn Garden City before the Second World War and was the Commonwealth War Graves Commission's architect for all their Second World War cemeteries in Italy, Greece and Austria. The forecourt is paved in marble and limestone, while pebbles are set in decorative patterns all around. A shelter, containing

An aerial view of the damage visited on Maleme airfield, in a photograph taken during a bombing raid by the RAF. A number of Ju-52s can be seen as having been wrecked and lay scattered about the area. There is also evidence of shell impact craters just to the right of centre. (Alexander Turnbull Library, DA-02059)

the register box and historical notice, sits on the left side of the cemetery and is made out of limestone, with a red tile roof. The cemetery is laid out symmetrically in 16 plots, with the memorial in the centre.

The German war cemetery is located near to Maleme, on Hill 107, where a large number of Germans were killed, with a memorial to the Fallschirmjäger just to the west of Hania on the coast road to Maleme. The cemetery was inaugurated on 6 October 1974 and contains the graves of 4,465 soldiers. The cemetery is divided into four areas associated with the main battlefields of Hania, Maleme, Rethymnon and Heraklion. Olive groves slope gently down to the west and the River Tavronitis. A set of steps leads up to the cemetery, which also has a number of benches, usually located in shady areas where one can sit and contemplate. Through an open hall, with a book containing the names of the dead, a path leads upwards to the graves, which are enclosed by walls. Each stone tablet contains the names of two servicemen, while in the centre of the cemetery lies a memorial square and the names of some 300 soldiers who were killed in the battle but whose remains could not be found. Many survivors helped with the work on the cemetery, and it is to the credit of the local population that they maintain the cemetery to the same high standard as the Allied cemetery in Souda Bay. Indeed, one of the first cemetery keepers was George Psychoundakis, a famous member of the Cretan resistance and the author of *The Cretan Runner*, a book translated by Patrick Leigh-Fermor. Many years after the war ended, he buried the remains of General Bruno Bräuer, which had been transferred to the German war cemetery from Athens at the request of the Association of German Airborne Troops. Both Bräuer and Müller had been sent back to Greece in 1946, to stand trial for war crimes that had allegedly been committed while they were in command in Crete, Müller being the most notorious for his brutality, Bräuer the least guilty of all. Both were sentenced to death. The date of the executions was distastefully delayed until the sixth anniversary of the invasion, 20 May 1947. Bräuer's death so shocked international opinion that Andrae and the other senior officers escaped with prison sentences.

Many other memorials to the fallen are scattered across the island at such places as Sphakion, Heraklion and Galatos. They include the RAF Memorial at Maleme, the Royal Artillery Memorial on the Akrotíri Peninsula, the Stavremenos Memorial to the Cretan resistance, and the Prevelli Monastery plaque that reads:

This region after the battle of Crete became the rallying point for hundreds of British, Australian and New Zealand soldiers, in defiance of ferocious German reprisals suffered by the monks and native population. They fed, protected and helped these soldiers to avoid capture and guided them to the beachhead where they escaped to the free world by British submarines.

A copy of *Crete News*, of which three editions were produced. The newspaper was edited by 2nd Lieutenant G. Cox who was a journalist in civilian life. It was an attempt by Freyberg to halt the spread of wild rumours. Cox managed to be evacuated on board the cruiser HMS *Perth*. (Alexander Turnbull Library, DA-06845)

ORDER OF BATTLE

Commonwealth and Allied Forces, Crete, May 1941

C-in-C, Commonwealth Forces, Middle East – General Sir Archibald Wavell
C-in-C, Mediterranean Fleet – Admiral Sir Andrew B. Cunningham
Air Officer C-in-C, Middle East – Air Chief Marshal Sir Arthur Longmore

HQ Creforce – Major-General Bernard Freyberg, VC (east of Hania)
'C' Squadron, the King's Own Hussars
'B' Squadron, 7th Royal Tank Regiment
1st Battalion, the Welch Regiment (Force Reserve)

HQ New Zealand Division – Brigadier Edward Puttick (west of Hania)
27th NZ MG Battalion
5th NZ Field Artillery Regiment

4th NZ Infantry Brigade – Brigadier L.M. Inglis (between Hania and Galatos)
18th NZ Infantry Battalion
19th NZ Infantry Battalion
20th NZ Infantry Battalion
1st Light Troop, Royal Artillery

5th NZ Infantry Brigade – Brigadier J. Hargest (Maleme and Platanias)
21st NZ Infantry Battalion
22nd NZ Infantry Battalion
23rd NZ Infantry Battalion
28th (Maori) Infantry Battalion
7th NZ Field Coy
19th Army Troops Coy
1st Greek Regiment

10th NZ Infantry Brigade – Colonel H.K. Kippenberger (around Galatos)
NZ Divisional Cavalry
NZ Composite Battalion
6th Greek Regiment
8th Greek Regiment

HQ 14th Infantry Brigade – Brigadier B.H. Chappel (Heraklion)
2nd Battalion, the Leicestershire Regiment
2nd Battalion, the York and Lancaster Regiment
2nd Battalion, the Black Watch
2/4 Australian Infantry Battalion
1st Battalion, Argyll & Sutherland Highlanders (Tymbaki)
7th Medium Regiment, RA (acting as infantry)
3rd Greek Regiment
7th Greek Regiment
Greek Garrison Battalion

HQ 19th Australian Infantry Brigade – Brigadier G.A. Vasey (at Georgioupolis, with LtCol I.R. Campbell commanding Rethymnon)
2/3 Field Artillery Regiment, RAA
2/1 Australian Infantry Battalion (Rethymnon)
2/11 Australian Infantry Battalion (Rethymnon)
2/7 Australian Infantry Battalion
2/8 Australian Infantry Battalion
4th Greek Regiment (Rethymnon)
5th Greek Regiment (Rethymnon)
Greek Gendarmerie (Rethymnon)

HQ Mobile Naval Base Defence Organisation – Major-General C.E. Weston, RM (Souda Bay)
15th Coastal Defence Regiment, RA
Royal Marine Battalion
1st Ranger Battalion (9th Battalion, King's Royal Rifle Corps)
Northumberland Hussars
106th Royal Horse Artillery
16th Australian Brigade Composite Battalion
17th Australian Brigade Composite Battalion
1st 'Royal Perivolian' Composite Battalion
2nd Greek Regiment

Axis Forces – Operation *Mercury*

HQ Luftflotte IV – General der Flieger Alexander Löhr
5th Panzer Division (Fehn)
6th Gebirgs Division (Schörner)

HQ Fliegerkorps VIII – General der Flieger Freiherr Wolfram von Richthofen
Kampfgeschwader 2 (Do-17Z)
Jagdgeschwader 77 (Bf 109E)
Lehrgeschwader 1 (Ju-88A & He-111H)
Sturzkampfgeschwader 1, 2 and 77 (Ju-87R)
Zerstörergeschwader 26 (Bf 110C & D)

HQ Fliegerkorps XI – Generalmajor Kurt Student
KGzbV 1, 2 and 3 (Ju-52)
22nd Luftlande Division (Sponeck) (in Romania)

HQ 7th Flieger Division – Generalleutnant Wilhelm Süssmann
(7th) Engineer, Artillery, Machine gun, Anti-tank, Anti-aircraft & Medical Bns.
1st Fallschirmjäger Regiment – Oberst Bruno Bräuer
1st Battalion – (Walther)
2nd Battalion – (Burckhardt)
3rd Battalion – (Schulz)

2nd Fallschirmjäger Regiment – Oberst Alfred Sturm
1st Battalion – (Kroh)
2nd Battalion – (Schirmer)
3rd Battalion – (Weidemann)

3rd Fallschirmjäger Regiment – Oberst Richard Heidrich
1st Battalion – (Heydte)
2nd Battalion – (Derpa)
3rd Battalion – (Heilmann)

HQ Luftlande Sturmregiment – Generalmajor Eugen Meindl
1st Battalion (Major W. Koch)
2nd Battalion (Major E. Stentzler)
3rd Battalion (Major O. Scherber)
4th Battalion (Hauptmann W. Gericke)

HQ 5th Gebirgs Division – Generalmajor Julius Ringel
(95th) Artillery, Anti-tank, Reconnaissance, Engineer & Signals Bns.
85th Gebirgsjäger Regiment (Krakau)
1st Battalion, 85th Gebirgsjäger Regiment
2nd Battalion, 85th Gebirgsjäger Regiment
3rd Battalion, 85th Gebirgsjäger Regiment

100th Gebirgsjäger Regiment (Utz)
1st Battalion, 100th Gebirgsjäger Regiment
2nd Battalion, 100th Gebirgsjäger Regiment
3rd Battalion, 100th Gebirgsjäger Regiment

141st Gebirgsjäger Regiment (Jais)
1st Battalion, 141st Gebirgsjäger Regiment
2nd Battalion, 141st Gebirgsjäger Regiment
3rd Battalion, 141st Gebirgsjäger Regiment

BIBLIOGRAPHY

Articles and Periodicals

Baldwin, Hanson W., 'Crete – Where Both Britain and Germany Erred', *Defence Journal*, September/October 1977 (Volume 3), pp. 34–47

Bell, Brig (Retd) A.T.J., 'The Battle for Crete – The Tragic Truth', *Australian Defence Force Journal*, May/June 1991, pp. 15–19

Brunskill, Brig G.S., 'The Administrative Aspect of the Campaign in Crete' *Army Quarterly*, July 1947, pp. 210–221

Falvey, Denis, 'The Battle for Crete – Myth and Reality', *Journal of the Society for Army Historical Research*, Summer 1993, pp. 119–126

Merriam, Ray (Ed.), 'Gebirgsjäger – Germany's Mountain Troops', *WWII Journal*, No. 9, (2003)

Murray, Williamson, 'Crete', *The Quarterly Journal of Military History*, Summer 1991, Volume 3, Number 4, pp. 28–35

Pallud, Jean. 'Operation *Merkur*: The German Invasion of Crete', *After The Battle*, No. 47, pp. 1–36

Pitt, Barrie (Ed.), 'How Crete was Lost', *History of the Second World War*, Volume 2, No. 3, Purnell & Sons Ltd, 1967

Books and Monographs

Beevor, Anthony, *Crete: The Battle and The Resistance*, Penguin Books (London, 1992)

Center of Military History, *The German Campaigns in the Balkans*, CMH Pub 104-4 (Washington DC, 1986)

Clark, Alan, *The Fall of Crete*, Cassell & Co. (London, 2001)

Davin, D.M., *Crete*, Official History of New Zealand in the Second World War 1939–45, War History Branch, Department of Internal Affairs (Wellington, 1953)

Ellis, Chris, *7th Flieger Division: Student's Fallschirmjäger Elite*, Ian Allan Publishing (Hersham, 2002)

Forbes, Dennis, *The Battle of Crete from the German View: Pyrrhic Victory or Unexploited Success?*, PhD Thesis, Department of History, Mississippi State University (USA, 1975)

Forty, George, *Battle for Crete*, Ian Allan Publishing (Hersham, 2001)

Lucas, James, *Alpine Elite*, Jane's Publishing Co. Ltd. (London, 1980)

Lucas, James, *Hitler's Commanders*, Cassell & Co. (London, 2000)

Lucas, James, *Hitler's Enforcers*, Cassell & Co. (London, 1996)

Lucas, James, *Storming Eagles*, Arms and Armour Press/Guild Publishing (London, 1988)

McDonald, Callum, *The Lost Battle – Crete 1941*, Papermac (London, 1995)

McNab, Chris, *German Paratroopers – The Illustrated History of the Fallschirmjäger in World War II*, Aurum Press (London, 2000)

Miller, Keith; Nicholls, Mark and Smurthwaite, David, *Touch and Go – The Battle for Crete 1941*, National Army Museum (London, 1991)

Quarrie, Bruce, *Fallschirmjäger: German Paratrooper 1935–45*, Warrior No. 38, Osprey Publishing (Oxford, 2001)

Quarrie, Bruce, *German Airborne Divisions: Blitzkrieg 1940–41*, Battle Orders No. 4, Osprey Publishing (Oxford, 2004)

Quarrie, Bruce, *German Airborne Troops 1939–45*, Men-At-Arms No. 139, Osprey Publishing (London, 1983)

Simpson, Tony, *Operation Mercury – The Battle for Crete, 1941*, Hodder and Stoughton (London, 1981)

Stewart, I., *The Struggle for Crete: A Story of Lost Opportunity*, Oxford University Press (London, 1966)

Williamson, Gordon, *Gebirgsjäger: German Mountain Trooper 1939–45*, Warrior No. 74, Osprey Publishing (Oxford, 2003).

Williamson, Gordon, *German Mountain & Ski Troops 1939–45*, Elite No. 63, Osprey Publishing (London, 1996)

INDEX

Hitler, Adolf 7–10, 12, 87
hospitals **24**, **25**, **60**, 83
Hungary 7, 8

Imbros Pass 85, 86
Inglis, Brig Lindsay 19, 21, 28, 35, 48, 64, 72, 73, 75, 80
intelligence flaws 34, 35, 36, 44, 87
Italian fleet 9, 18, **35**, 36, 62
Italy 7, 8–9, 17, 28, 88

Ju-52 13, **14**, 20, **30**, 31, 33, **36**, 37, 40, **40**, **41**, **45**, **48**, 49, **49**, **51**, **54–5**, 56, **58**, 60, **91**
Ju-87R 31

Kampfgruppe
   Ramcke 65, 69, 72, 75, 80
   Wittmann **31**, 77, 81, 83, 84
Kaso Strait 82
Kastelli 41, 65, 68, 69, 83
Kippenberger, LtCol Howard 18–19, **18**, 35, 48, 72
Knight's Cross 22, 23, 59
Koch, Major Walter 22–3, 30, 40, **41**
Kommitades 86
Kroh, Major 49, 51, 61

Laycock, Col Robert 73
Layforce 73, 77, 83
Lerapetra 84
Libya 7, 9
Löhr, Gen Alexander 20, 32, 36, 58
Luftflotte IV 31, 32, 36
Luftlande Sturmregiment 21, 22, 23, 30, 33, 37, 41, **41**, **42–3**, 44, 45, 48, 53, **53**, 59, 60, **60**, 62, 64, 65
Luftwaffe losses **36**, 37, 40, **40**, **41**, 44, 45, **49**, **53**, **54–5**, 56, 87

Mackay, MajGen Sir Iven 12, 27
Maleme 22, **30**, 34, 35, 62, 69, **91**, 92
   assault on 20, 21, 25, 32, 33, 37, **38–9**, 40, **40**, 41, 45, 53, 56, 58, **58**, 59, 60, 63, 64, 65, **66–7**, 68, **68**, **91**
   counterattack **38–9**, **52**, 62, 63–5
   defence of **38–9**, 40, 41, **41**, 45, 51, **52**, **53**, 58–9, 60, 62, 63–5, **68**
   withdrawal from **38–9**, 58–9
Malta 12, 18, 29
Megala Khorafia 77
Meindl, Generalmajor Eugen 21, 30, 33, 41, 60
Mersa Matruh 8, 90
Metaxas Line 29
Milos island 62
Modi village 65
Moir, Sgt Tom **89**
mortars 75, 77, 80
Morzik, Oberst **36**
motorcycles **31**, 77
Müller, Friedrich-Wilhelm 89, 90, 92
Mürbe, Leutnant Peter 41, 69
Mussolini (Il Duce) 7, 8, 29

Neapolis 88
New Zealand forces **6**, **9–10,** 12, **13–15**, 17–20, **25**, 27, 28, **28**, 40, 72, **76**, 93

battalions **10**, 18, 19, 20, 28, **28**, 35, **36**, 40, 41, 45, 48, **52**, **53**, 58, 62, 63, 64–5, 72, 77, 84, **84**
brigades **12**, 18, **18**, 19, 28, **28**, 35, 48, **50**, 61, 62, 65, 69, 72, 73, 76, 77, **78–9**, 80, 84, 86, **88**
divisions 12, 27, 28, 35, 48, 51, 68, 72, **75**, **84**, 91
regiments 28, **28**
North Africa 8, 12

O'Connor, MajGen Richard 12, 17, 27
Operation *Merkur* (Mercury)
   chronology 15–16
   historical significance 7
   invasion plans 32–4, 36, 87
   Order of Battle 93
   timetable slippage 37, 48, 49

Paleochora 68
parachutes 34, **54–5**, 56, **63**
paradrops **42–3**, 44, 45, **45**, 48–9, **48**, **49**, **50**, 51–2, **51**, 53, **54–5**, 56, 57, 60, **60**, 61, 62, 69
paratroopers 7, 12, 13, **14**, 21, 25, 29–30, **30**, 31, **31**, 33, **34**, 37, **37**, 40–1, **40**, **41**, **42–3**, 44, 45, **45**, 48–9, **48**, **49**, **50**, **51**, 52–3, **52**, **53**, **54–5**, 56, 57, **58**, 59, **59**, 60, **60**, 61, **61**, 62, 65, **72**, 82, 83, 87
Perivolia 49, 61, **61**, 73, 83
Pink Hill/Valley 48, 61
Piraeus harbour 62
Platanias
   assault on 65, **66–7**, 68
   counterattack 65, **66–7**
   defence of 65, **66–7**
Plessen, Oblt Wulf von 40, 57
Porto Rafti **9**
Prison Valley 22, 33, 48, **48**, 57
   assault on 37, **46**, 56, 60–1
   defence of 46, 61
prisoners 57, **60**, 75, **77**, 82, **85**, 87
Puttick, Brig Edward 18, 28, 48, 64, 69, 73, 75, 80, 85
Pyrgos village 60, 64, 65

Raeder, Grossadmiral Erich 7, 12
RAF 9, 41, 87, 88, **89**
Ramcke, Oberst Bernhard 21–2, 60, 64, 65, 75
Rethymnon 32, 33, 34, 35, 58, 76, 77, 88, 91, 92
   assault on **47**, 49, 56, 61, 83–4
   civilian resistance 49
   counterattack **47**, 51, 61
   defence of **47**, 49, 51, 61, 64, 83, 84
Ringel, Generalmajor Julius **14**, 21, **21**, 31, 33, 65, 76, 77, 80, 83
Romania (oilfields) 7, 8, 31
Rommel, Generalleutnant Erwin 12
Royal Navy 18, 29, 73, **77**, 81, **81**
   evacuations **12**, 18, 29, 82–3, **84**, 85, 86, **88**
   interceptions 24, 31, 33, **35**, 62–3
   and Italian fleet 9, 18
   losses 29, 63, **81**, 82–3, 87
   and Luftwaffe 31, 62, 63, 87

Royal Perivolians 63, 75

Schätte, Major 65, 68
Scherber, Major Otto 23, 40, 45, 60, 65
Schirmer, Hptm Gerhard 56, 57
Schulz, Hptm Karl-Lothar 53, 56, 57, 62
Schuster, Konteradmiral Karl-Georg 33
seaborne threat 33, 34, 36, 62–3
ships **9**, 12, **12**, **28**, 29, 33, 35, **35**, 62, 63, **77**, **81**, 82–3, **84**, 85, 86, 87, **88**, **92**
Sitia 84, 88
Skarpanto island 82
SOE agents 89, 90
Souda/Souda Bay **17**, 22, 33, 34, 35, **35**, 36, 44, **52**, **75**, 76, 80, 81, 91
   Allied forces **9**, **25**, **46**
   German advance 9, **46**, 75, 77
Southern Dobrudja 8
Soviet Union 7, 8, 10, 12
Spanish Republicans 77
Sphakion
   advance to **74**, 84–5, 86
   evacuation **15**, 36, 76, **76**, 77, 84–5
   retreat 73, **74**, 76–7, 83
Spilia 41, 83
Stalos 65
Stavromenos 61
Stentzler, Major Edgar 41, 58
Stilos 77, 81
Student, Generalmajor Kurt 7, 20–1, **20**, 21, 30, 31, 32, 48, 58, 59–60, 68, 87, 88
Sturm, Oberst Alfred 12, 30, 33, 49, 56
Suez Canal 7, 8, 12, 27
Süssmann, Generalleutnant Willhelm 30, 33, 37

tanks 12, 13, 24, **26**, 45, 48, 51, **54–5**, 56, 61, **63**, 64, **68**, 69, 72, 81, 83, 85
transit camps **35**
Tripartite Pact 12

'Ultra' intercepts 36, **48**, 62, 88
Upham, Lt Charles **18**, **19**

Vasey, Brig George Alan 19, 27, 35, 64, 72, 73, 76–7, 80, 84
Victoria Cross **18**, **19**
Vlaheronitissa 65
Von der Heydte, Hauptmann 23
Von Richthofen, General 21, 31, **33**, 87

'W' Force 12, **13**, 27, **28**, 29
Walker, Lt Col Theo 64, 86, 87
Walther, Major Erich 53, 56
war crimes 22, 92
Wavell, Gen Sir Archibald 12, 17, **17**, **19**, **33**, 34, 75, 76, 86, 88
Weston, Maj Gen Eric **26**, 27, 35, 73, 75, 76, 80, 85
Wilson, Gen Henry 12
Witzig, Hptm Rudolf 23

Yugoslavia 7, 12, 13